Light and Tasty Cooking Labs

100 Eating-Smart Preparations

Jean Bunnell

Illustrations by Paola Lazzaro

J. WESTON
WALCH
PUBLISHER

PORTLAND, MAINE

1   2   3   4   5   6   7   8   9   10

ISBN 0-8251-1505-1

Copyright © 1989
J. Weston Walch, Publisher
P.O. Box 658 • Portland, Maine 04104-0658

Printed in the United States of America

Contents

♂	Indicates easiest recipes
🍒	Indicates recipes that require more cooking skills
🍒	Indicates most involved recipes
2	Indicates recipes that can be adapted to a 2-day lab

Main Dishes

Main Dishes (*continued*)

Soups

Sandwiches

Sandwiches (*continued*)

Meats

Vegetables and Salads

Vegetables And Salads (*continued*)

Salad Dressings And Dips

Breads

To the Teacher

With today's increasing emphasis on health and good eating, many teenagers are becoming more interested in their diets. This group of 100 recipes provides you with a wide variety of healthful recipes to use with your classes. Recipes are divided into nine categories: main dishes, soups, sandwiches, meats, vegetables, dressings and dips, breads, beverages, and desserts.

Recipes in this collection have been chosen to appeal to teenagers, including such standard favorites as spaghetti, hero sandwiches, and potato chips. Care has been taken to use low-cost and readily available ingredients. Recipes are for small amounts (most make four servings) to encourage maximum student involvement in preparing each dish.

Some recipes are very easy and can be prepared by beginning cooks. These are indicated with a ♂. Recipes requiring a little more cooking skill are marked with ♣ . The most involved recipes are shown with ♣♣ . While all the dishes can be prepared in under an hour, some of the more complex recipes can be split into 2-day labs. These recipes are indicated by a ⬚2⬚ and specific instructions are included on the *Teacher Preparation Sheet*.

Each recipe is accompanied by a *Student Activity Sheet* which includes a list of ingredients and utensils needed. Clear, step-by-step directions are given. A blank line beside each direction encourages students in cooking groups to plan who will take responsibility for each step in completing the recipe.

The *Teacher Preparation Sheet* for each recipe features a shopping list. Amounts of each item to purchase are listed for classes of 16, 20, 24, 28, and 32 students. Notes are included for any necessary pre-class preparation. Suggestions are also given for ways to divide responsibilities among members of the cooking groups.

Beyond the specific recipes, an additional goal of this book is to help students learn to prepare healthy foods. Skills and techniques used in preparing the dishes in this book can be applied to other recipes. The chart on page *xiv* offers ideas for choosing and adapting recipes for better health. Since abbreviations for measures are used throughout, a reproducible chart of abbreviations is included on page *xv*. Feel free to make as many copies as you need.

How to Use This Book

When selecting a recipe to use with your class, consider these questions:

■ Is it a recipe your students will enjoy making and eating? Many teenagers have quite limited food preferences. You may need to choose very traditional recipes for them. Other students will enjoy trying a larger variety of recipes and experimenting with foods new to them.

■ Do your students have enough cooking experience to complete the recipe successfully? Students come with a wide range of cooking skills. Some have been cooking since they could hold a mixing spoon. Others have trouble opening the wrapper on a frozen dinner. To help you select recipes that match your students' abilities, each recipe is marked according to difficulty. ♂ recipes are the easiest. ♂♂ recipes will require more cooking skills. ♂♂♂ recipes are most involved.

■ Are students familiar with all the cooking vocabulary and preparation methods? Note which items will need explanation and demonstration when you go over the recipe with your students the day before they actually cook. You may want to make the recipe ahead of time at home so you can advise students of any potential trouble areas.

■ Is there enough class time to complete the recipe? While all the recipes can be prepared in under an hour, classroom realities often slow things down. Depending on the abilities and concentration levels of your students, some of the more involved recipes may be best completed over two days. These recipes are marked with a ⬚2⬚ and specific suggestions are given for dividing the preparation steps.

■ Are ingredients readily available in your area? Every effort has been made to include only ingredients that are widely available. If you do not have easy access to a particular ingredient, consider using a substitute ingredient, or avoid using that recipe with your class.

■ Will the expense of the ingredients fit your budget? Try to coordinate your choice of recipe with what is being featured in the grocery stores. If chicken is on sale, select a chicken recipe. Use recipes calling for fruits or vegetables that are in season.

■ What utensils are available in your cooking lab? A list of needed utensils is given with each recipe. Again, there is some flexibility. A skillet may be substituted for a wok. Perhaps a fork or spoon would work as well as a whisk. Be flexible and adapt recipes to your situation.

Photocopy the recipe. Make a copy for each student.

On the class day before cooking day, go over the recipe with your students. This will allow students to start cooking immediately at the beginning of the class period on cooking day.

- Distribute copies of the recipe.
- Read the recipe together, explaining terms and demonstrating methods and techniques as necessary.
- Divide the students into cooking groups. A group of four students cooking together usually gives everyone a chance to get involved in preparation. However, you may have to alter the number of students in a group, depending on your situation.
- Help the students decide who should be responsible for each step of the recipe. They can use the blank line beside each direction to assign responsibility for each step. To help you with this, a suggested division of responsibilities is listed on each *Teacher Preparation Sheet*. (Note that several steps can often be done simultaneously by several students. For example, in preparing spaghetti, someone can start the pasta while others are making the sauce. Or, if several vegetables need to be prepared, students can each work to prepare one of the vegetables. Point out to students ways in which they can efficiently divide the tasks.)
- If you are splitting the recipe into a 2-day lab, explain to students what will be done on which day.
- Assign clean-up duties.
- Collect the recipes at the end of the period. This will ensure that all the recipe sheets get to class on cooking day!

Shop for necessary ingredients.

- With each recipe, there is a complete shopping list that indicates how much of each ingredient you will need to purchase. Amounts are given for classes having from four to eight cooking groups.
- Some items, such as spices, flour, etc., may be on hand in your cooking lab. Check the cupboards before you buy unnecessary ingredients.
- Perishable items will need to be purchased specifically for class.
- You may not be able to buy the exact amount specified in the shopping list. For example, if a recipe calls for $\frac{1}{4}$ lemon and you have 5 cooking groups, the shopping list will indicate $1\frac{1}{4}$ lemons. Obviously you would have to purchase 2 whole lemons.
- Make substitutions or additions to the recipes as needed or desired. If you have an overstock of green beans, by all means substitute them for the vegetable specified in the recipe. If you do not have a garlic press, use powdered garlic or garlic granules. If your students turn green at the thought of spinach pasta, use plain. Feel free to adapt the recipes so they will best fit your situation.

Before class:

■ Do any cooking ahead as may be indicated on the *Teacher Preparation Sheet*. When it is necessary for the teacher to cook any ingredients before class, it is highlighted with a ⟨Cook⟩ .

■ Divide ingredients as indicated on the *Teacher Preparation Sheet* and distribute to the individual cooking groups.

■ Some ingredients, such as molasses, soy sauce, or juice concentrate, would be messy to divide, so make the containers available to all the cooking groups in a central location. Students can then measure their own ingredients from the original containers.

On cooking day:

■ Return recipe sheets to the students.

■ Supervise "cooks," offering suggestions and encouragement when necessary.

■ Sample the finished products.

■ Discuss with students their results. Did they have trouble with any part of the recipe? How was the result? Would they make changes in the recipe if they prepared it again? What might be served with this dish?

Some variations for using the recipes in this book:

■ Have each member of the groups work independently to make one item of a complete menu. For instance, one student could make spaghetti, another could make bread, a third student might make a salad, and a fourth student could prepare dessert. By the end of class, each group will have a complete meal for four people. Some suggested menus are given on the following page; students can also create their own menus.

■ With more capable students who do not need much supervision, try a "Sampler Day." Have each group make a different recipe—then all the groups can share samples of the foods they have prepared. This strategy works particularly well with salad dressings. One group might prepare ingredients for a tossed salad bar. Other groups could make different kinds of dressings. Students could each have a salad and try the different dressings. Try a "Sampler Day" with dip recipes, breads, or even main dishes or desserts!

Menu Suggestions

Using the Recipes in This Book

Menu #1

Spaghetti (p. 34)
Tossed Salad
with Vinaigrette Dressing (p. 156)
Orange Nog (p. 186)
Chocolate Angel Food Cupcakes (p. 200)

Menu #2

Egg Drop Soup (p. 62)
Sesame-Oat Crackers (p. 172)
Oriental Beef and
Vegetable Stir-Fry (p. 27)
Crunchy Fruit Parfait (p. 206)

Menu #3

Meal in a Packet (p. 25)
Blueberry Muffins (p. 164)
Iced Apple-Mint Tea (p. 184)
Citrus Cups (p. 202)

Menu #4

Pita Hero (p. 86)
Baked Potato Chips (p. 110)
T. J. Pizzazz (p. 192)
Granola Cookies (p. 212)

Menu #5

Stuffed Shells (p. 38)
Parmesan Steamed Vegetables (p. 124)
Cranberry Punch (p. 180)
Light Chocolate Mousse (p. 218)

Menu #6

Corn Chowder (p. 60)
Apple-Tuna Toasts (p. 76)
Hot Tomato Bouillon (p. 182)
Tropical Fruit Bowl (p. 224)

Menu #7

Tuna Loaf (p. 104)
Greek Potato Salad (p. 118)
Herb-Baked Tomatoes (p. 120)
Hot-Fudge Sundae (p. 214)

Menu #8

Rainbow Slaw (p. 128)
Chicken Tacos (p. 80)
with Salsa (p. 150)
Pink Drinks (p. 190)

Menu #9

Salad with
Cucumber-Herb Dressing (p. 144)
Chili (p. 58)
Whole-Wheat Corn Muffins (p. 174)
Baked Apples (p. 196)

Menu #10

Fish and Spinach Pie (p. 17)
Cottage-Cheese Biscuits (p. 168)
Cucumber-Orange Salad (p. 114)
Fruit Tarts (p. 208)

Beverages

Desserts

Choosing and Adapting Recipes for Better Health

Instead of . . .	Try . . .
choosing recipes that emphasize meats	selecting stir-fry or soup recipes that feature vegetables
salt	herbs or spices
sautéing vegetables (onions, celery, etc.) in margarine or butter	softening vegetables in a little water
sour cream	low-fat yogurt or cottage cheese
frying in oil	boiling, poaching, or baking
red meat	fish or chicken
using slices of cheese	grating the cheese so less will go further
including whipped cream in desserts	beating egg whites to add lightness to desserts
adding sugar for sweetness	using the natural sweetness of fruit juice or fruit-juice concentrates
selecting cookies or other sugary treats	snacking on fruit or raw vegetables
using fruits packed in heavy syrup	choosing fruits packed in their own juices
whole milk	skim milk or low-fat milk

A Chart of Abbreviations

These are abbreviations of commonly used measurements. Most cookbooks will use these abbreviations, or variations of them.

Abbreviation	Measurement
gal	gallon
" (2", 4", etc.)	inch
oz	ounce
pt	pint
lb	pound
qt	quart
tbsp	tablespoon
tsp	teaspoon

Note that the abbreviations are the same in the singular as in the plural: 2 tbsp, 1 pt, 6½ oz, etc.

Main Dishes

Teacher Preparation Sheet

Banana Pancakes with Strawberry Sauce

SHOPPING LIST

(4 students per group)	16 students	20 students	24 students	28 students	32 students
old-fashioned oats	$1\frac{1}{3}$ cups	$1\frac{2}{3}$ cups	2 cups	$2\frac{1}{3}$ cups	$2\frac{2}{3}$ cups
skim milk	3 cups	$3\frac{3}{4}$ cups	$4\frac{1}{2}$ cups	$5\frac{1}{4}$ cups	$1\frac{1}{2}$ qt
ripe bananas	2	$2\frac{1}{2}$	3	$3\frac{1}{2}$	4
eggs	4	5	6	7	8
vegetable oil	2 oz	$2\frac{1}{2}$ oz	3 oz	$3\frac{1}{2}$ oz	4 oz
flour	$2\frac{2}{3}$ cups	$3\frac{1}{3}$ cups	4 cups	$4\frac{2}{3}$ cups	$5\frac{1}{3}$ cups
baking powder	2 tsp	$2\frac{1}{2}$ tsp	3 tsp	$3\frac{1}{2}$ tsp	4 tsp
margarine	2 tsp	$2\frac{1}{2}$ tsp	3 tsp	$3\frac{1}{2}$ tsp	4 tsp
frozen strawberries	16 oz	20 oz	24 oz	28 oz	32 oz
orange juice	$1\frac{1}{3}$ cups	$1\frac{2}{3}$ cups	2 cups	$2\frac{1}{3}$ cups	$2\frac{2}{3}$ cups

A suggested division of responsibilities

Student A: steps 1, 2, 5, 11
Student B: steps 3, 4, 6, 12
Student C: steps 7, 8, 9, 10
Student D: steps 15, 16, 17
All students take part in steps 13, 14, 18

Before class

1. Divide oats into $\frac{1}{3}$-cup packages.
2. Cut bananas in half.
3. Provide 1 egg for each group.
4. Divide frozen strawberries into 4-oz packages.

NOTES

1. Students can measure skim milk, vegetable oil, flour, baking powder, margarine, and orange juice from original containers.
2. Other frozen fruit or juices can be substituted in the sauce.

Banana Pancakes with Strawberry Sauce

Makes 4 Servings

Directions

Ingredients

$\frac{1}{3}$ cup old-fashioned oats

$\frac{3}{4}$ cup skim milk

$\frac{1}{2}$ ripe banana

1 egg

$\frac{2}{3}$ cup flour

$\frac{1}{2}$ tsp baking powder

$\frac{1}{2}$ tsp margarine

4 oz frozen strawberries

$\frac{1}{3}$ cup orange juice

1 tsp vegetable oil

Utensils

2 small bowls

measuring cup

fork

mixing spoon

measuring spoons

large bowl

non-stick skillet

spatula

blender

_____ 1. Measure $\frac{1}{3}$ cup **oats** into bowl.

_____ 2. Measure $\frac{3}{4}$ **cup skim milk** into the bowl with the oats. Let stand 5 minutes.

_____ 3. Peel $\frac{1}{2}$ **banana**. Put banana in small bowl and mash it.

_____ 4. Add **banana** to the oat mixture.

_____ 5. Break an **egg** into the oat mixture.

_____ 6. Measure **1 tbsp oil** into the oat mixture.

_____ 7. Measure $\frac{2}{3}$ **cup flour** into large bowl.

_____ 8. Measure $\frac{1}{2}$ **tsp baking powder** into the bowl with the flour. Mix.

_____ 9. Add **oat mixture** to the flour and baking powder.

_____ 10. Stir until just blended.

_____ 11. Heat skillet.

_____ 12. Lightly grease skillet with the **margarine**.

_____ 13. Pour 2-3 tbsp batter onto the skillet for each pancake. Batter will make 8 pancakes.

_____ 14. Cook over medium heat. When tops bubble and edges brown, turn pancakes to cook second side.

_____ 15. Put **strawberries** in the blender.

_____ 16. Measure $\frac{2}{3}$ **cup orange juice** into blender.

_____ 17. Put cover on blender. Blend until smooth.

_____ 18. Pour strawberry sauce over pancakes.

Cabbage Rolls

SHOPPING LIST

(4 students per group)	16 students	20 students	24 students	28 students	32 students
cabbage	32 leaves	40 leaves	48 leaves	56 leaves	64 leaves
onions	4	5	6	7	8
vegetable oil	2 oz	$2\frac{1}{2}$ oz	3 oz	$3\frac{1}{2}$ oz	4 oz
brown rice	1 lb	$1\frac{1}{4}$ lb	$1\frac{1}{2}$ lb	$1\frac{3}{4}$ lb	2 lb
sunflower seeds	1 cup	$1\frac{1}{4}$ cups	$1\frac{1}{2}$ cups	$1\frac{3}{4}$ cups	2 cups
cheddar cheese	8 oz	10 oz	12 oz	14 oz	16 oz
8-oz cans tomato sauce	4 cans	5 cans	6 cans	7 cans	8 cans
Worcestershire sauce	8 tsp	10 tsp	2 oz	14 tsp	16 tsp

2 **To use this recipe in a 2-day lab**
- On day 1, complete steps 1-14.
  Cover and refrigerate the stuffed cabbage leaves.
- On day 2, complete steps 15-20.

A suggested division of responsibilities
Student A: steps 1, 2, 3, 4, 15
Student B: steps 5, 6, 7, 16
Student C: steps 8, 9, 17
Student D: steps 10, 11, 18, 19, 20
All students take part in steps 12, 13, 14

NOTES
1. Students can measure vegetable oil and Worcestershire sauce directly from their original containers.
2. Students can measure cooked rice from the pot it is cooked in.
3. Left-over cabbage can be used in *Ginger Pork and Cabbage* on page 21.

Before class
1. Provide a cabbage or 4 cabbage leaves for each group. If the cabbage leaves do not easily separate from the cabbage, soak the whole head in hot water for a few minutes.
2. Provide each group with an onion.
Cook 3. Cook the brown rice. Bring water to a boil. Add rice. Cover tightly and cook over low heat until all water is absorbed (about 50 minutes). To make 8 cups rice, use 1 lb of brown rice and $4\frac{2}{3}$ cups water.
4. Divide sunflower seeds into $\frac{1}{4}$-cup pkgs.
5. Provide each group with a 2-oz wedge of cheese.
6. Provide each group with a can of tomato sauce.

Cabbage Rolls

Makes 4 Servings		**Directions**

<table>
<tr><td>

Ingredients

1 medium cabbage

1 onion

1 tbsp vegetable oil

2 cups cooked brown rice

$\frac{1}{4}$ **cup sunflower seeds**

2 oz cheddar cheese

1 8-oz can tomato sauce

2 tsp Worcestershire sauce

</td></tr>
</table>

Utensils

saucepan with cover
cutting board
paring knife
skillet with cover
measuring spoons
wooden spoon
cheese grater
8 toothpicks
can opener
small bowl

_____ 1. Remove 8 large leaves from **cabbage**.

_____ 2. Place cabbage leaves in saucepan and just cover with water.

_____ 3. Cook leaves in boiling water 5 to 6 minutes or until just tender.

_____ 4. Remove cabbage leaves from water.

_____ 5. Peel **onion**. Chop onion and put in skillet.

_____ 6. Add **1 tbsp vegetable oil** to skillet.

_____ 7. Cook onions over medium heat until softened, stirring constantly. Remove from heat.

_____ 8. Add **2 cups cooked brown rice** to skillet.

_____ 9. Add $\frac{1}{4}$ **cup sunflower seeds** to skillet.

_____ 10. Grate **cheese**.

_____ 11. Add grated cheese to rice mixture and stir.

_____ 12. Place $\frac{1}{3}$ cup rice mixture in center of each cabbage leaf.

_____ 13. Fold sides of cabbage over rice mixture and roll up each leaf.

_____ 14. Hold cabbage leaf in place with a toothpick.

_____ 15. Place cabbage rolls in skillet.

_____ 16. Pour **tomato sauce** into bowl.

_____ 17. Measure **2 tsp Worcestershire sauce** into bowl and mix.

_____ 18. Pour tomato sauce mixture over cabbage rolls.

_____ 19. Bring to a boil.

_____ 20. Reduce heat. Cover and simmer 10 minutes.

Chicken Kabobs

SHOPPING LIST

(4 students per group)	16 students	20 students	24 students	28 students	32 students
chicken breasts	4	5	6	7	8
reduced-calorie Italian salad dressing	8 oz	10 oz	12 oz	14 oz	16 oz
soy sauce	2 oz	$2\frac{1}{2}$ oz	3 oz	$3\frac{1}{2}$ oz	4 oz
lemon juice	4 tsp	5 tsp	6 tsp	7 tsp	8 tsp
ground ginger	1 tsp	$1\frac{1}{4}$ tsp	$1\frac{1}{2}$ tsp	$1\frac{3}{4}$ tsp	2 tsp
garlic	4 cloves	5 cloves	6 cloves	7 cloves	8 cloves
medium onions	4	5	6	7	8
green peppers	4	5	6	7	8
cherry tomatoes	48	60	72	84	96

2 **To use this recipe in a 2-day lab:**
- On day 1, complete steps 1-15.
  Cover each of the ingredients and refrigerate.
- On day 2, complete steps 16 and 17.

A suggested division of responsibilities

Student A: steps 1, 10, 11, 12, 13
Student B: steps 2, 9
Student C: steps 3, 4, 5, 6, 14
Student D: steps 7, 8, 15
All students take part in steps 16 and 17

NOTES
1. Students can measure salad dressing, soy sauce, lemon juice, and ground ginger from their original containers.
2. If using wooden skewers, soak them in water at least $\frac{1}{2}$ hour ahead of time to prevent burning.

Before class

1. Provide each group with 1 whole chicken breast.
2. Provide each group with a garlic clove.
3. Provide each group with 1 medium onion.
4. Provide each group with a green pepper.
5. Provide each group with 12 cherry tomatoes.

Chicken Kabobs

Makes 4 Servings

Directions

Ingredients

1 whole chicken breast

$\frac{1}{4}$ **cup reduced-calorie Italian salad dressing**

1 tbsp soy sauce

1 tsp lemon juice

$\frac{1}{4}$ **tsp ground ginger**

1 garlic clove

1 medium onion

1 green pepper

12 cherry tomatoes

Utensils

sharp knife

cutting board

shallow soup bowl

large jar with lid

measuring cup

measuring spoons

garlic press

mixing spoon

small sauce pan

slotted spoon

4 skewers

baking sheet

_____ 1. Preheat oven to broil.

_____ 2. Remove skin and bones from **chicken breast**. Cut chicken into 1″ pieces. Place chicken in soup bowl.

_____ 3. Measure $\frac{1}{4}$ **cup reduced-calorie Italian salad dressing** into the jar.

_____ 4. Measure **1 tbsp soy sauce** into the jar.

_____ 5. Measure **1 tsp lemon juice** into the jar.

_____ 6. Measure $\frac{1}{4}$ **tsp ground ginger** into the jar.

_____ 7. Peel **garlic clove** and crush. Add to jar.

_____ 8. Put jar cover on tightly and shake well to make the marinade.

_____ 9. Pour marinade over the chicken. Stir frequently to coat all the chicken.

_____ 10. Half fill the saucepan with water. Bring to a boil.

_____ 11. Peel the **onion**. Cut into 8 wedges.

_____ 12. Add the onion wedges to the boiling water. Parboil for 2 minutes.

_____ 13. Use a slotted spoon to remove the onion from the water.

_____ 14. Cut the **green pepper** into $1\frac{1}{2}″$ squares.

_____ 15. Wash the **cherry tomatoes** and remove stems.

_____ 16. Alternately thread chicken, onion, tomato, and green pepper onto the skewers. Place skewers on a baking sheet.

_____ 17. Broil 10-12 minutes. Turn frequently.

Chow Mein with Tuna

SHOPPING LIST

(4 students per group)	16 students	20 students	24 students	28 students	32 students
onions	4	5	6	7	8
celery	24 stalks	30 stalks	36 stalks	42 stalks	48 stalks
bamboo shoots	4 cans	5 cans	6 cans	7 cans	8 cans
4-oz cans mushrooms	4 cans	5 cans	6 cans	7 cans	8 cans
15-oz cans bean sprouts	4 cans	5 cans	6 cans	7 cans	8 cans
soy sauce	2 oz	$2\frac{1}{2}$ oz	3 oz	$3\frac{1}{2}$ oz	4 oz
molasses	2 oz	$2\frac{1}{2}$ oz	3 oz	$3\frac{1}{2}$ oz	4 oz
cornstarch	$\frac{1}{2}$ cup	10 tbsp	$\frac{3}{4}$ cup	14 tbsp	1 cup
$6\frac{1}{2}$-oz cans tuna, water-packed	4 cans	5 cans	6 cans	7 cans	8 cans

A suggested division of responsibilities

Student A: steps 1, 5, 13

Student B: steps 2, 6, 7

Student C: steps 3, 4, 14

Student D: steps 8, 9, 10, 11, 12

All students take part in step 15

NOTES

1. Students can measure water, soy sauce, molasses, and cornstarch from their original containers.

2. Students could sprout their own bean sprouts to use in this recipe if they were started 5 days to a week ahead of time.

Before class

1. Provide each group with an onion.

2. Provide each group with 6 stalks of celery.

3. Provide each group with 1 can bamboo shoots.

4. Provide each group with a can of mushrooms.

5. Provide each group with a can of bean sprouts.

6. Provide each group with a can of tuna.

Chow Mein With Tuna

Makes 4 Servings

Directions

Ingredients
1 onion
6 stalks celery
1 can bamboo shoots
1 4-oz can mushrooms
1 15-oz can bean sprouts
$\frac{1}{2}$ **cup water**
1 tbsp soy sauce
1 tbsp molasses
2 tbsp cornstarch
1 6$\frac{1}{2}$-oz can tuna (packed in water)

1. Peel **onion**. Slice onion and put in skillet.
2. Trim **celery**. Cut on the diagonal. Add to skillet.
3. Add 2 or 3 tbsp water to the skillet.
4. Cook onion and celery over medium heat, stirring constantly, until vegetables are softened.
5. Drain **1 can bamboo shoots** and add to skillet.
6. Drain can of **mushrooms** and add to skillet.
7. Drain **bean sprouts** and add to skillet.
8. Measure $\frac{1}{2}$ **cup water** into small mixing bowl.
9. Measure **1 tbsp soy sauce** into mixing bowl.
10. Measure **1 tbsp molasses** into mixing bowl.
11. Measure **2 tbsp cornstarch** into mixing bowl.
12. Stir sauce ingredients and add to skillet.
13. Cook about 5 minutes until hot and sauce thickens.
14. Add **tuna** and heat through.
15. Serve over hot rice.

Utensils

cutting board
paring knife
skillet
wooden spoon
can opener
small mixing bowl
measuring cup
measuring spoons
mixing spoon

Corn Frittata

SHOPPING LIST

(4 students per group)	16 students	20 students	24 students	28 students	32 students
margarine	4 tbsp	5 tbsp	6 tbsp	7 tbsp	1 stick
green onions	8	10	12	14	16
8-oz cans whole-kernel corn	4 cans	5 cans	6 cans	7 cans	8 cans
eggs	16	20	24	28	32
skim milk	1 cup	$1\frac{1}{4}$ cups	$1\frac{1}{2}$ cups	$1\frac{3}{4}$ cups	2 cups
dried basil	2 tsp	$2\frac{1}{2}$ tsp	3 tsp	$3\frac{1}{2}$ tsp	4 tsp
black pepper	4 dashes	5 dashes	6 dashes	7 dashes	8 dashes
small tomatoes	8	10	12	14	16
cheddar cheese	8 oz	10 oz	12 oz	14 oz	16 oz

A suggested division of responsibilities

Student A: steps 1, 4, 12
Student B: steps 2, 3, 13, 14, 15
Student C: steps 5, 9, 10, 11
Student D: steps 6, 7, 8

NOTES

1. Students can measure skim milk, basil, and black pepper from their original containers.

2. Students can vary this recipe with different vegetables to make their own frittata recipes.

Before class

1. Provide each group with 1 tbsp margarine.

2. Provide each group with 2 green onions.

3. Provide each group with a can of corn.

4. Provide each group with 4 eggs.

5. Provide each group with 2 small tomatoes.

6. Divide cheese into 2-oz wedges for each group.

Corn Frittata

Makes 4 Servings

Ingredients

1 tbsp margarine

2 green onions

1 8-oz can whole-kernel corn

4 eggs

$\frac{1}{4}$ **cup skim milk**

$\frac{1}{2}$ **tsp dried basil**

dash black pepper

2 small tomatoes

2 oz cheddar cheese

Utensils

cutting board

paring knife

non-stick 10″ skillet with cover

measuring spoons

measuring cup

small bowl

fork

cheese grater

can opener

Directions

_____ 1. Measure **1 tbsp margarine** into skillet. Melt.

_____ 2. Trim **2 green onions**. Chop into small pieces.

_____ 3. Add chopped green onion to skillet. Sauté until soft.

_____ 4. Drain can of **corn**. Add corn to skillet. Stir.

_____ 5. Break **4 eggs** into small bowl. Beat with a fork.

_____ 6. Measure $\frac{1}{4}$ **cup skim milk** into the bowl.

_____ 7. Measure $\frac{1}{2}$ **tsp basil** into the bowl.

_____ 8. Sprinkle with **black pepper**.

_____ 9. Mix ingredients in the bowl.

_____ 10. Pour egg mixture over corn mixture in the skillet.

_____ 11. Cover and cook over low heat until mixture is almost set (about 10 minutes).

_____ 12. Cut **tomatoes** into thin wedges. Place around edge of egg mixture.

_____ 13. Grate **cheese**.

_____ 14. Sprinkle cheese over the frittata.

_____ 15. Cover and cook 2 to 3 minutes longer until cheese melts.

Crêpes

SHOPPING LIST

(4 students per group)	16 students	20 students	24 students	28 students	32 students
flour	2 cups	$2\frac{1}{2}$ cups	3 cups	$3\frac{1}{2}$ cups	4 cups
skim milk	$1\frac{1}{2}$ qt	$7\frac{1}{2}$ cups	9 cups	$10\frac{1}{2}$ cups	3 qt
eggs	4	5	6	7	8
broccoli	4 stems	5 stems	6 stems	7 stems	8 stems
small onions	2	$2\frac{1}{2}$	3	$3\frac{1}{2}$	4
cornstarch	$\frac{1}{2}$ cup	10 tbsp	$\frac{3}{4}$ cup	14 tbsp	1 cup
Swiss cheese	12 oz	15 oz	18 oz	21 oz	24 oz
4-oz cans mushrooms	4 cans	5 cans	6 cans	7 cans	8 cans
chicken drumsticks and thighs	12	15	18	21	24
black pepper	$\frac{1}{2}$ tsp	$\frac{5}{8}$ tsp	$\frac{3}{4}$ tsp	$\frac{7}{8}$ tsp	1 tsp
margarine	$\frac{1}{2}$ stick	5 tbsp	6 tbsp	7 tbsp	1 stick

2 To use this recipe in a 2-day lab

- On day 1, complete steps 1-22. Cover the crêpe mixture, the filling, and the sauce.
- On day 2, complete steps 23-31.

A suggested division of responsibilities

Student A: steps 1, 2, 3, 4, 5, 6, 23
Student B: steps 7, 8, 9, 18, 19
Student C: steps 10, 11, 12, 13, 14, 15, 16, 17
Student D: steps 20, 21, 22
All students take part in steps 24, 25, 26, 27, 28, 29, 30, 31

NOTES

1. Students can measure flour, skim milk, cornstarch, and black pepper from their original containers.
2. Crêpes can be used with a variety of fillings. They are great for making leftovers a little fancier. Or try filling with fruit for a sweet treat.

Before class

Cook 1. Cook chicken drumsticks and thighs. Provide 3 of each for each group.
2. Provide 1 egg for each group.
3. Provide 1 stem broccoli for each group.
4. Cut onions in half and provide $\frac{1}{2}$ onion for each group.
5. Divide cheese into 3-oz wedges and distribute to each group.
6. Provide a can of mushrooms for each group.
7. Provide 1 tbsp margarine for each group.

Crêpes

Makes 4 Servings

Directions

Ingredients

$\frac{1}{2}$ **cup flour**

$\frac{3}{4}$ **cup skim milk**

1 egg

1 stem broccoli

$\frac{1}{2}$ **small onion**

2 tbsp cornstarch

$\frac{3}{4}$ **cup skim milk**

3 oz Swiss cheese

4-oz can mushrooms

3 cooked chicken drumsticks and thighs

$\frac{1}{8}$ **tsp black pepper**

1 tbsp margarine

_____ 1. Preheat oven to 350°.

_____ 2. Measure $\frac{1}{2}$ **cup flour** into blender.

_____ 3. Measure $\frac{3}{4}$ **cup skim milk** into blender.

_____ 4. Break **egg** into blender.

_____ 5. Cover blender and blend until smooth.

_____ 6. Let batter set, allowing flour particles to swell and soften so crêpes will be light.

_____ 7. Remove tough part of **broccoli** stem. Cut broccoli into bite-sized pieces and put in saucepan.

_____ 8. Just cover broccoli with water.

_____ 9. Cover saucepan and cook broccoli over medium heat 10-12 minutes.

_____ 10. Peel **onion**. Chop and put in small saucepan.

_____ 11. Add 2-3 tbsp water to saucepan.

_____ 12. Cook over medium heat, stirring constantly, until onion is softened.

_____ 13. Sprinkle **2 tbsp cornstarch** over onion.

_____ 14. Stirring constantly, gradually add $\frac{3}{4}$ **cup skim milk** to the saucepan.

_____ 15. Cook and stir until sauce thickens.

_____ 16. Grate **cheese** and add to milk mixture.

_____ 17. Stir until cheese melts. Remove from heat.

_____ 18. Drain broccoli.

_____ 19. Drain **mushrooms** and add to broccoli.

_____ 20. Remove skin and bones from **chicken**. Cut chicken into bite-sized pieces and add to broccoli.

_____ 21. Add $\frac{1}{8}$ **tsp black pepper** to mixture.

(continued)

Crêpes (*continued*)

| **Utensils** | **Directions** (*continued*) |

measuring cup

_____ 22. Add half the cheese sauce to the broccoli-chicken mixture and stir all ingredients gently.

blender

cutting board

_____ 23. Lightly grease heated skillet with **margarine**.

paring knife

saucepan with cover

_____ 24. Pour 2 tbsp crêpe batter into the pan and tilt pan so batter covers the bottom.

small saucepan

measuring spoons

_____ 25. Cook 1 minute. Crêpe is ready to flip when it can be shaken loose from the pan.

wooden spoon

cheese grater

_____ 26. Flip crêpe and cook 30 seconds longer.

can opener

_____ 27. Make 8 crêpes.

6″ skillet or crêpe pan

13″ x 9″ baking dish

_____ 28. Spoon about $\frac{1}{4}$ cup filling on the unbrowned side of each crêpe and roll up.

aluminum foil

_____ 29. Put crêpes in baking dish.

_____ 30. Cover with aluminum foil and bake 15-20 minutes until heated through.

_____ 31. Serve warm with remaining cheese sauce.

Curried Rice with Chicken and Peas

SHOPPING LIST

(4 students per group)	16 students	20 students	24 students	28 students	32 students
chicken thighs and drumsticks	8	10	12	14	16
shallots	24	30	36	42	48
curry powder	8 tsp	10 tsp	12 tsp	14 tsp	16 tsp
chicken bouillon	$\frac{1}{4}$ cup	5 tbsp	6 tbsp	7 tbsp	$\frac{1}{2}$ cup
long-grain rice (uncooked)	4 cups	5 cups	6 cups	7 cups	8 cups
tomato juice	16 oz	20 oz	24 oz	28 oz	32 oz
frozen peas	4 cups	5 cups	6 cups	7 cups	8 cups

A suggested division of responsibilities

    Student A: steps 1, 2, 13, 14, 15

    Student B: steps 3, 4, 9, 16

    Student C: steps 5, 7, 10, 11, 17

    Student D: steps 6, 8, 12

Before class

1. Provide 2 chicken drumsticks and thighs for each group.

2. Provide 6 shallots for each group.

3. Divide rice into 1-cup packets.

4. Divide frozen peas into 1-cup packets.

NOTES

1. Students can measure curry powder, chicken bouillon, water, and tomato juice from the original containers.

2. A variety of other vegetables can be substituted for the peas. Tuna or beef could be used instead of chicken.

Curried Rice with Chicken and Peas

Makes 4 Servings

Directions

Ingredients
2 chicken drumsticks and thighs
6 shallots
2 tsp curry powder
1 tbsp chicken bouillon
1 cup long-grain rice
1$\frac{1}{2}$ cups water
$\frac{1}{2}$ cup tomato juice
1 cup frozen peas

Utensils

saucepan with cover
paring knife
cutting board
wok or skillet with cover
wooden spoon
measuring spoons
measuring cup
fork

_____ 1. Remove skin from **chicken**.

_____ 2. Place chicken in saucepan. Cover chicken with water. Put cover on pan and let cook over medium heat 25 minutes until tender.

_____ 3. Peel **shallots**. Chop and put in wok.

_____ 4. Add 2-3 tbsp water to wok and cook over medium-high heat, stirring constantly, until shallots are softened.

_____ 5. Measure **2 tsp curry powder** into wok. Stir.

_____ 6. Measure **1 tbsp chicken bouillon** into wok. Stir.

_____ 7. Measure **1 cup rice** into wok.

_____ 8. Measure **1$\frac{1}{2}$ cups water** into wok.

_____ 9. Measure **$\frac{1}{2}$ cup tomato juice** into wok.

_____ 10. Bring mixture in wok to a boil.

_____ 11. Stir once, cover, and simmer over low heat 20 minutes until rice is tender and liquid is nearly absorbed.

_____ 12. Add **1 cup peas** to the wok. Cook 4-5 minutes.

_____ 13. Remove chicken from bones.

_____ 14. Cut chicken into bite-sized pieces.

_____ 15. Add chicken to rice mixture.

_____ 16. Remove wok from heat, cover and let stand 2 or 3 minutes until chicken is heated through.

_____ 17. Fluff rice with a fork and serve hot.

16

Fish and Spinach Pie

SHOPPING LIST

(4 students per group)	16 students	20 students	24 students	28 students	32 students
margarine	2 tsp	$2\frac{1}{2}$ tsp	3 tsp	$3\frac{1}{2}$ tsp	4 tsp
fish (fresh or frozen)	4 lb	5 lb	6 lb	7 lb	8 lb
eggs	8	10	12	14	16
10-oz pkgs. frozen spinach	4	5	6	7	8
green onions	8	10	12	14	16
Parmesan cheese	$\frac{1}{2}$ cup	10 tbsp	$\frac{3}{4}$ cup	14 tbsp	1 cup
powdered nutmeg	$\frac{1}{2}$ tsp	$\frac{5}{8}$ tsp	$\frac{3}{4}$ tsp	$\frac{7}{8}$ tsp	1 tsp
black pepper	4 dashes	5 dashes	6 dashes	7 dashes	8 dashes

A suggested division of responsibilities

Student A: steps 1, 4, 5
Student B: steps 2, 3, 13, 14
Student C: steps 6, 7, 11
Student D: steps 8, 9, 10, 12

Before class

1. Provide each group with 1 lb of fish.
2. Provide each group with 2 eggs.
3. Provide each group with a package of spinach.
4. Provide each group with 2 green onions.

NOTE

1. Students can measure margarine, Parmesan cheese, nutmeg, and black pepper from the original containers.

Fish and Spinach Pie

Makes 4 Servings

Directions

Ingredients

$\frac{1}{2}$ **tsp margarine**

**1 lb fish, fresh or frozen
(e.g., haddock, cod,
sole, perch)**

2 eggs

**1 10-oz package frozen
spinach (defrosted)**

2 green onions

**2 tbsp grated
Parmesan cheese**

$\frac{1}{8}$ **tsp nutmeg**

dash of black pepper

Utensils

saucepan
fork
9″ pie pan
paper towel
bowl
cutting board
paring knife
measuring spoons

_____ 1. Preheat oven to 400°.

_____ 2. Place **fish** in saucepan. Cover with water.

_____ 3. Simmer fish 5 to 10 minutes or until it flakes easily with a fork. Do not overcook. Drain the fish.

_____ 4. Use a paper towel to grease the pie plate with $\frac{1}{2}$ **tsp margarine.**

_____ 5. Break fish into flakes and place in the pie pan.

_____ 6. Break **2 eggs** into a bowl. Use a fork to mix well.

_____ 7. Add **spinach** to the eggs.

_____ 8. Wash and chop **2 green onions**. Add to bowl.

_____ 9. Measure **2 tbsp Parmesan cheese** into the bowl.

_____ 10. Measure $\frac{1}{8}$ **tsp nutmeg** into the bowl.

_____ 11. Sprinkle with **black pepper.**

_____ 12. Mix all ingredients well.

_____ 13. Pour egg mixture over flaked fish.

_____ 14. Bake for 20 minutes.

French Toast

SHOPPING LIST

(4 students per group)	16 students	20 students	24 students	28 students	32 students
eggs	8	10	12	14	16
skim milk	2 cups	$2\frac{1}{2}$ cups	3 cups	$3\frac{1}{2}$ cups	1 qt
frozen apple-juice concentrate	6 oz	$7\frac{1}{2}$ oz	9 oz	$10\frac{1}{2}$ oz	12 oz
vanilla extract	2 tsp	$2\frac{1}{2}$ tsp	3 tsp	$3\frac{1}{2}$ tsp	4 tsp
ground cinnamon	4 tsp	5 tsp	6 tsp	7 tsp	8 tsp
ground cloves	1 tsp	$1\frac{1}{4}$ tsp	$1\frac{1}{2}$ tsp	$1\frac{3}{4}$ tsp	2 tsp
whole-wheat bread	16 slices	20 slices	24 slices	28 slices	32 slices
margarine	2 tsp	$2\frac{1}{2}$ tsp	3 tsp	$3\frac{1}{2}$ tsp	4 tsp
unsweetened apple-sauce	16 oz	20 oz	24 oz	28 oz	32 oz

A suggested division of responsibilities

Student A: steps 1, 2, 10

Student B: steps 3, 4, 5, 6

Student C: steps 7, 8, 9

Student D: steps 14, 15, 16

All students take part in steps 11, 12, 13

Before class

1. Provide each group with 2 eggs.

2. Provide each group with 4 slices whole-wheat bread.

NOTE

1. Students can measure skim milk, apple-juice concentrate, vanilla extract, cinnamon, cloves, margarine, and applesauce from the original containers.

French Toast

Makes 4 Servings

Directions

<table>
<tr><td></td><td>Ingredients</td></tr>
</table>

Ingredients
2 eggs
$\frac{1}{2}$ **cup skim milk**
3 tbsp apple-juice concentrate
$\frac{1}{2}$ **tsp vanilla extract**
$\frac{1}{2}$ **tsp cinnamon**
$\frac{1}{4}$ **tsp cloves**
4 slices whole-wheat bread
$\frac{1}{2}$ **tsp margarine**
$\frac{1}{2}$ **cup unsweetened apple-sauce**
$\frac{1}{2}$ **tsp cinnamon**

Utensils

soup bowl
fork
measuring cup
measuring spoons
non-stick skillet
spatula
small bowl
mixing spoon

_____ 1. Break **2 eggs** into shallow soup bowl.

_____ 2. Use a fork to beat eggs well.

_____ 3. Measure $\frac{1}{2}$ **cup skim milk** into the bowl with the eggs.

_____ 4. Measure **3 tbsp apple-juice concentrate** into the bowl.

_____ 5. Measure $\frac{1}{2}$ **tsp vanilla** into the bowl.

_____ 6. Mix liquid ingredients together.

_____ 7. Sprinkle $\frac{1}{2}$ **tsp cinnamon** over liquid ingredients.

_____ 8. Sprinkle $\frac{1}{4}$ **tsp nutmeg** over liquid ingredients.

_____ 9. Mix well.

_____ 10. Heat skillet. Lightly grease skillet with $\frac{1}{2}$ **tsp margarine**.

_____ 11. One at a time, dip **bread** slices into the egg mixture coating well.

_____ 12. Cook over medium heat 3-4 minutes until light brown.

_____ 13. Turn bread and cook until brown on second side.

_____ 14. Measure $\frac{1}{2}$ **cup unsweetened applesauce** into small bowl.

_____ 15. Measure $\frac{1}{2}$ **tsp cinnamon** into the applesauce.

_____ 16. Mix well and serve over the French toast.

Ginger Pork and Cabbage

SHOPPING LIST

(4 students per group)	16 students	20 students	24 students	28 students	32 students
pork chops	8	10	12	14	16
large onions	4	5	6	7	8
chicken-flavored bouillon granules	4 tsp	5 tsp	6 tsp	7 tsp	8 tsp
soy sauce	2 oz	$2\frac{1}{2}$ oz	3 oz	$3\frac{1}{2}$ oz	4 oz
powdered ginger	2 tbsp	$7\frac{1}{2}$ tsp	3 tbsp	$10\frac{1}{2}$ tsp	4 tbsp
cornstarch	$\frac{1}{2}$ cup	10 tbsp	$\frac{3}{4}$ cup	14 tbsp	1 cup
cabbage	2 heads	$2\frac{1}{2}$ heads	3 heads	$3\frac{1}{2}$ heads	4 heads

A suggested division of responsibilities

    Student A: steps 1, 2, 3
    Student B: steps 4, 5, 6
    Student C: steps 7, 8, 9, 10, 11, 12
    Student D: steps 13, 14, 15, 16

Before class

1. Provide each group with 2 pork chops.

2. Provide each group with an onion.

3. Cut cabbage heads in half and provide each group with $\frac{1}{2}$ head.

NOTE

  1. Students can measure water, bouillon, soy sauce, ginger, and cornstarch from the original containers.

Ginger Pork and Cabbage

Makes 4 Servings

Directions

Ingredients

2 pork chops

large onion

$\frac{1}{2}$ **cup water**

1 tsp chicken-flavored bouillon granules

1 tbsp soy sauce

$1\frac{1}{2}$ tsp powdered ginger

2 tbsp corn starch

$\frac{1}{2}$ **head cabbage**

Utensils

cutting board

sharp knife

non-stick skillet with cover

wooden spoon

paper towel

small mixing bowl

mixing spoon

_____ 1. Cut bones away from **2 pork chops**. Cut meat into small cubes.

_____ 2. Heat skillet. Cook pork over medium heat, stirring constantly.

_____ 3. When meat is no longer pink, remove from pan and drain on paper towel.

_____ 4. Peel **onion**. Slice onion and put in skillet.

_____ 5. Add 2-3 tbsp water to skillet.

_____ 6. Cook over medium heat, stirring constantly, until onion is softened.

_____ 7. Measure $\frac{1}{2}$ **cup water** into small mixing bowl.

_____ 8. Measure **1 tsp chicken bouillon** into mixing bowl.

_____ 9. Measure **1 tbsp soy sauce** into mixing bowl.

_____ 10. Measure **$1\frac{1}{2}$ tsp ginger** into mixing bowl.

_____ 11. Measure **2 tbsp cornstarch** into mixing bowl.

_____ 12. Mix sauce together in small mixing bowl and add to skillet.

_____ 13. Remove core from **cabbage** and chop cabbage.

_____ 14. Add cabbage to skillet. Stir thoroughly and cook 10-12 minutes over medium heat until cabbage is cooked.

_____ 15. Return pork to skillet and heat through.

_____ 16. Serve with rice.

Light and Tasty Cooking Labs

Kasha-Tuna Combo

SHOPPING LIST

(4 students per group)	16 students	20 students	24 students	28 students	32 students
buckwheat groats	1 lb	$1\frac{1}{4}$ lb	$1\frac{1}{2}$ lb	$1\frac{3}{4}$ lb	2 lb
eggs	8	10	12	14	16
small onions	4	5	6	7	8
red bell peppers	2	$2\frac{1}{2}$	3	$3\frac{1}{2}$	4
margarine	$\frac{1}{2}$ stick	5 tbsp	6 tbsp	7 tbsp	1 stick
chicken bouillon	$\frac{1}{2}$ cup	10 tbsp	$\frac{3}{4}$ cup	14 tbsp	1 cup
$6\frac{1}{2}$-oz cans tuna	4 cans	5 cans	6 cans	7 cans	8 cans
medium tomatoes	4	5	6	7	8

A suggested division of responsibilities

Student A: steps 1, 2, 6

Student B: steps 3, 7

Student C: steps 4, 8

Student D: steps 5, 9

NOTES

1. Students can measure bouillon and hot water from the original containers.

2. Buckwheat groats (kasha) are available in health-food stores as well as in a growing number of super-markets.

Before class

1. Divide buckwheat groats into 1-cup packages.

2. Provide each group with 2 eggs.

3. Provide each group with a small onion.

4. Cut red peppers in half and give each group $\frac{1}{2}$ pepper.

5. Cut margarine into 1-tbsp pieces and give a piece to each group.

6. Provide each group with a can of tuna.

7. Provide each group with a tomato.

Kasha-Tuna Combo

Makes 4 Servings

Directions

Ingredients

1 cup uncooked buckwheat groats (kasha)

2 eggs

1 small onion

$\frac{1}{2}$ **red bell pepper**

1 tbsp margarine

2 tbsp chicken bouillon

$1\frac{1}{2}$ **cups hot water**

1 6$\frac{1}{2}$-oz can of tuna

1 medium tomato

_____ 1. In a small bowl, mix together **1 cup uncooked buckwheat groats** and **2 eggs**.

_____ 2. Heat non-stick skillet. Add groats-egg mixture and cook, stirring constantly. Cook until mixture is dry and grains are separated. Reduce heat to low.

_____ 3. Peel **1 small onion**. Chop and add to skillet.

_____ 4. Remove seeds from $\frac{1}{2}$ **red bell pepper**. Dice pepper and add to skillet.

_____ 5. Add **1 tbsp margarine** to skillet. Stir to mix all ingredients.

_____ 6. Sprinkle **2 tbsp chicken bouillon** over mixture.

_____ 7. Add $1\frac{1}{2}$ **cups hot water** to mixture. Cover skillet and cook 8 to 10 minutes until liquid has been absorbed.

_____ 8. Open and drain **1 6$\frac{1}{2}$-oz. can of tuna**. Add to skillet.

_____ 9. Remove core and dice **1 medium tomato**. Add to skillet. Heat, stirring occasionally.

Utensils

small bowl

measuring cup

wooden spoon

cutting board

paring knife

skillet (non-stick) & cover

measuring spoons

can opener

Meal in a Packet

SHOPPING LIST

(4 students per group)	16 students	20 students	24 students	28 students	32 students
white fish, fresh or frozen	4 lb	5 lb	6 lb	7 lb	8 lb
broccoli	4 stems	5 stems	6 stems	7 stems	8 stems
carrots	4	5	6	7	8
green onions	8	10	12	14	16
lemons	2	$2\frac{1}{2}$	3	$3\frac{1}{2}$	4
garlic powder	2 tsp	$2\frac{1}{2}$ tsp	3 tsp	$3\frac{1}{2}$ tsp	4 tsp
dried dillweed	2 tsp	$2\frac{1}{2}$ tsp	3 tsp	$3\frac{1}{2}$ tsp	4 tsp

A suggested division of responsibilities

Student A: steps 1, 5
Student B: steps 2, 6
Student C: steps 3, 4, 7
Student D: steps 8, 9, 10, 11, 12
All students take part in steps 13, 14, 15

Before class

1. Provide each group with 1 lb of fish.
2. Provide each group with a stem of broccoli.
3. Provide each group with a carrot.
4. Provide each group with 2 green onions.
5. Cut lemons in half and give half a lemon to each group.

NOTES

1. Students can measure garlic powder and dillweed from the original containers.
2. Parchment paper can be used instead of aluminum foil.

Meal in a Packet

Makes 4 Servings

Directions

Ingredients

1 lb white fish
(e.g., cusk, halibut,
haddock)

1 large stem broccoli

1 carrot

2 green onions

$\frac{1}{2}$ **lemon**

$\frac{1}{2}$ **tsp garlic powder**

$\frac{1}{2}$ **tsp dried dillweed**

Utensils

aluminum foil

sharp knife

cutting board

vegetable peeler

vegetable grater

measuring spoons

small bowl

spoon

baking sheet

_____ 1. Preheat oven to 450°.

_____ 2. Cut 4 pieces of aluminum foil 12″ x 18″.

_____ 3. Cut **fish** into 4 pieces.

_____ 4. Place one piece of fish on each piece of foil.

_____ 5. Cut flowerets from the **broccoli**. Top each piece of fish with one-fourth of the broccoli flowerets.

_____ 6. Peel the **carrot**. Use vegetable grater to shred the carrot. Divide shredded carrot among the 4 foil packages.

_____ 7. Trim and chop the **green onions**. Add to the foil packages.

_____ 8. Squeeze the **lemon**. Put the juice in the small bowl.

_____ 9. Measure $\frac{1}{2}$ **tsp garlic powder** into the bowl.

_____ 10. Measure $\frac{1}{2}$ **tsp dillweed** into the bowl.

_____ 11. Stir the lemon mixture.

_____ 12. Spoon one-fourth of the lemon mixture over each package of vegetables and fish.

_____ 13. Fold the foil over each package of vegetables and fish. Wrap loosely, leaving space for air circulation and expansion. Seal the edges together.

_____ 14. Place the packages on a baking sheet.

_____ 15. Bake 10-15 minutes or until fish flakes.

Oriental Beef and Vegetable Stir-Fry

SHOPPING LIST

(4 students per group)	16 students	20 students	24 students	28 students	32 students
vermicelli	24 oz	30 oz	36 oz	42 oz	48 oz
ground beef	4 lb	5 lb	6 lb	7 lb	8 lb
teriyaki sauce	4 oz	5 oz	6 oz	7 oz	8 oz
ginger root	4″	5″	6″	7″	8″
garlic	8 cloves	10 cloves	12 cloves	14 cloves	16 cloves
frozen peas	4 cups	5 cups	6 cups	7 cups	8 cups
beef bouillon	$\frac{1}{2}$ cup	10 tbsp	$\frac{3}{4}$ cup	14 tbsp	1 cup
soy sauce	2 oz	$2\frac{1}{2}$ oz	3 oz	$3\frac{1}{2}$ oz	4 oz
cornstarch	$\frac{1}{4}$ cup	5 tbsp	6 tbsp	7 tbsp	$\frac{1}{2}$ cup
scallions	8	10	12	14	16

A suggested division of responsibilities

Student A: steps 1, 2, 3, 13

Student B: steps 4, 7, 11, 12

Student C: steps 5, 8, 9

Student D: steps 6, 10, 14, 15

NOTES

1. Students can measure teriyaki sauce, beef bouillon, soy sauce, and cornstarch directly from their original containers.

2. Students can use either a skillet or a wok for cooking this dish.

3. Other vegetables, such as green beans or broccoli, can be substituted for the peas.

Before class

1. Divide vermicelli into 6-oz packages.

2. Divide ground beef into 1-lb packages.

3. Cut a section of ginger root for each group of students.

4. Separate 2 gloves of garlic for each group.

5. Divide frozen peas into 1-cup packages.

6. Provide 2 scallions for each cooking group.

Oriental Beef and Vegetable Stir-Fry

Makes 4 Servings

Directions

Ingredients

**6 oz vermicelli
(very thin spaghetti)**

2 qt water

1 lb ground beef

2 tbsp teriyaki sauce

1″ piece ginger root

2 cloves garlic

1 cup frozen peas

1$\frac{1}{2}$ cups water

2 tbsp beef bouillon

1 tbsp soy sauce

1 tbsp cornstarch

$\frac{1}{2}$ cup scallions

Utensils

large kettle
wooden spoon
colander
skillet or wok
measuring cup
measuring spoons
garlic press
bowl
small mixing bowl
cutting board
paring knife
paper towel

_____ 1. Put **2 qt water** in large kettle. Bring water to a boil.

_____ 2. Add **6 oz vermicelli** to boiling water. Boil uncovered 6 minutes. Stir occasionally.

_____ 3. Drain vermicelli in a colander.

_____ 4. Chop ginger root to make 2 tsp.

_____ 5. Put garlic cloves through garlic press.

_____ 6. In a bowl, combine **1 lb ground beef, 2 tbsp teriyaki sauce, 2 tsp ginger root,** and **2 cloves garlic**. Mix well.

_____ 7. Brown beef in skillet. Stir while cooking.

_____ 8. Drain beef on paper towel. Return beef to pan.

_____ 9. Add **1 cup frozen peas** and **1 cup water** to beef in skillet. Stir constantly and cook two minutes.

_____ 10. Add $\frac{1}{2}$ **cup water** and **2 tbsp beef bouillon** to skillet.

_____ 11. In a small mixing bowl, combine **1 tbsp soy sauce** and **1 tbsp cornstarch**. Stir to dissolve cornstarch.

_____ 12. Add soy sauce-cornstarch mixture to skillet. Stir constantly until thickened.

_____ 13. Add vermicelli to skillet. Mix gently.

_____ 14. Chop 2 or 3 scallions to make $\frac{1}{2}$ **cup chopped scallions.**

_____ 15. Sprinkle individual servings with scallions.

Pasta Salad

SHOPPING LIST

(4 students per group)	16 students	20 students	24 students	28 students	32 students
spinach corkscrew pasta	1 lb	20 oz	24 oz	28 oz	2 lb
chicken franks	12	15	18	21	24
celery	8 stalks	10 stalks	12 stalks	14 stalks	16 stalks
red pepper	1	$1\frac{1}{4}$	$1\frac{1}{2}$	$1\frac{3}{4}$	2
carrots	4	5	6	7	8
green onions	4	5	6	7	8
reduced-calorie mayonnaise	6 oz	$7\frac{1}{2}$ oz	9 oz	$10\frac{1}{2}$ oz	12 oz
plain low-fat yogurt	6 oz	$7\frac{1}{2}$ oz	9 oz	$10\frac{1}{2}$ oz	12 oz
Dijon mustard	8 tsp	10 tsp	4 tbsp	14 tsp	16 tsp
black pepper	1 tsp	$1\frac{1}{4}$ tsp	$1\frac{1}{2}$ tsp	$1\frac{3}{4}$ tsp	2 tsp

A suggested division of responsibilities

Student A: steps 1, 2, 3, 4, 5, 11
Student B: steps 6, 7, 8, 12
Student C: steps 9, 13, 14, 15, 16
Student D: steps 10, 17, 18, 19

NOTES

1. Students can measure mayonnaise, yogurt, mustard, and black pepper from the original containers.

2. A variety of different pastas can be used in this recipe. Your students may prefer plain pasta. Try other shapes as well.

Before class

1. Divide pasta into 4-oz packages.

2. Provide each group with 3 chicken franks.

3. Provide each group with 2 stalks celery.

4. Cut red peppers into quarters and give 1 piece to each group.

5. Provide each group with 1 carrot.

6. Provide each group with a green onion.

Pasta Salad

Makes 4 Servings

Directions

Ingredients

4 oz spinach corkscrew pasta

3 chicken franks

2 stalks celery

$\frac{1}{4}$ red pepper

1 carrot

1 green onion

3 tbsp reduced-calorie mayonnaise

3 tbsp plain low-fat yogurt

2 tsp Dijon mustard

$\frac{1}{4}$ tsp black pepper

Utensils

large saucepan
wooden spoon
colander
2 mixing bowls
non-stick skillet
paring knife
cutting board
vegetable peeler
grater
measuring spoons
mixing spoon

_____ 1. Half fill large saucepan with water. Heat to a boil.

_____ 2. Add **4 oz spinach pasta**.

_____ 3. Stirring occasionally, cook pasta over low heat 10-12 minutes. Cooked pasta should be still firm.

_____ 4. Drain pasta in colander. Rinse with cold water.

_____ 5. Put pasta in large bowl.

_____ 6. Slice **franks**.

_____ 7. Heat skillet.

_____ 8. Cook frank slices, turning frequently to keep from burning. Add to bowl.

_____ 9. Trim **celery**. Chop and add to bowl.

_____ 10. Remove seeds from **red pepper**. Chop and add to bowl.

_____ 11. Peel **carrot**. Grate and add to bowl.

_____ 12. Trim **green onion**. Chop and add to bowl.

_____ 13. Measure **3 tbsp reduced-calorie mayonnaise** into small bowl.

_____ 14. Measure **3 tbsp yogurt** into small bowl.

_____ 15. Measure **2 tsp mustard** into small bowl.

_____ 16. Measure **$\frac{1}{4}$ tsp black pepper** into small bowl.

_____ 17. Mix dressing ingredients together in small bowl.

_____ 18. Add dressing to large bowl.

_____ 19. Gently mix salad ingredients.

Pork and Apple Stir-Fry

SHOPPING LIST

(4 students per group)	16 students	20 students	24 students	28 students	32 students
long-grain white rice	$2\frac{2}{3}$ cups	$3\frac{1}{3}$ cups	4 cups	$4\frac{2}{3}$ cups	$5\frac{1}{3}$ cups
pork chops	8	10	12	14	16
ground cinnamon	1 tsp	$1\frac{1}{4}$ tsp	$1\frac{1}{2}$ tsp	$1\frac{3}{4}$ tsp	2 tsp
ground cloves	1 tsp	$1\frac{1}{4}$ tsp	$1\frac{1}{2}$ tsp	$1\frac{3}{4}$ tsp	2 tsp
ground nutmeg	1 tsp	$1\frac{1}{4}$ tsp	$1\frac{1}{2}$ tsp	$1\frac{3}{4}$ tsp	2 tsp
cornstarch	$\frac{1}{2}$ cup	10 tbsp	$\frac{3}{4}$ cup	14 tbsp	1 cup
unsweetened apple juice	$1\frac{1}{3}$ cups	$1\frac{2}{3}$ cups	2 cups	$2\frac{1}{3}$ cups	$2\frac{2}{3}$ cups
soy sauce	2 oz	$2\frac{1}{2}$ oz	3 oz	$3\frac{1}{2}$ oz	4 oz
cider vinegar	2 oz	$2\frac{1}{2}$ oz	3 oz	$3\frac{1}{2}$ oz	4 oz
apples	8	10	12	14	16
8-oz cans pineapple chunks, juice-packed	4 cans	5 cans	6 cans	7 cans	8 cans

A suggested division of responsiblities

Student A: steps 1, 2, 3, 4, 5, 6

Student B: steps 7, 17, 18, 19

Student C: steps 8, 9, 10, 11, 12, 13, 14, 15

Student D: steps 16, 20, 21, 22, 23, 24, 25

Before class

1. Divide rice into $\frac{2}{3}$-cup packets.

2. Provide each group with 2 pork chops.

3. Provide each group with 2 apples.

4. Provide each group with an 8-oz can of pineapple chunks.

NOTE

1. Students can measure water, cinnamon, cloves, nutmeg, cornstarch, apple juice, soy sauce, and vinegar from the original containers.

Pork and Apple Stir-Fry

Makes 4 Servings

Directions

Ingredients

$\frac{2}{3}$ **cup long-grain white rice**

1$\frac{1}{4}$ cups water

2 pork chops

$\frac{1}{4}$ **tsp cinnamon**

$\frac{1}{4}$ **tsp cloves**

$\frac{1}{4}$ **tsp nutmeg**

2 tbsp cornstarch

$\frac{1}{3}$ **cup unsweetened apple juice**

1 tbsp soy sauce

1 tbsp cider vinegar

2 cooking apples

1 8-oz can pineapple chunks (juice-packed)

Utensils

saucepan with cover
measuring cup
wooden spoon
cutting board
sharp knife
measuring spoons
small bowl
non-stick skillet

_____ 1. Measure **1$\frac{1}{4}$ cups water** into saucepan. Bring to boil.

_____ 2. Measure $\frac{2}{3}$ **cup rice** into the boiling water.

_____ 3. Stir rice and cover.

_____ 4. When water is boiling again, stir rice. Cover tightly and turn off heat.

_____ 5. Leave rice covered for 20 minutes until liquid is absorbed.

_____ 6. If liquid remains after 20 minutes, return to heat and cook 2 to 4 minutes longer.

_____ 7. Remove **pork** from bones. Slice pork into very thin strips.

_____ 8. Measure $\frac{1}{4}$ **tsp cinnamon** into small bowl.

_____ 9. Measure $\frac{1}{4}$ **tsp cloves** into small bowl.

_____ 10. Measure $\frac{1}{4}$ **tsp nutmeg** into small bowl.

_____ 11. Measure **2 tbsp cornstarch** into small bowl.

_____ 12. Gradually add $\frac{1}{3}$ **cup apple juice** to the spice mixture, stirring to mix well.

_____ 13. Measure **1 tbsp soy sauce** into the bowl.

_____ 14. Measure **1 tbsp vinegar** into the bowl.

_____ 15. Open can of **pineapple chunks**. Drain juice into small bowl. Mix all ingredients in small bowl and set aside.

_____ 16. Cut **apples** in quarters. Remove cores. Slice apples.

_____ 17. Heat skillet over medium heat.

(continued)

Pork and Apple Stir-Fry (*continued*)

Directions (*continued*)

_____ 18. Add pork and cook, stirring continuously until pork is browned.

_____ 19. Remove pork from skillet.

_____ 20. Put apple slices in skillet. Stir constantly and cook about 3 minutes until apples start to brown.

_____ 21. Return pork to skillet.

_____ 22. Add pineapple chunks to skillet.

_____ 23. Add juice and spice mixture to skillet.

_____ 24. Heat, stirring constantly, about 2 minutes or until sauce thickens.

_____ 25. Serve hot over rice.

Spaghetti

SHOPPING LIST

(4 students per group)	16 students	20 students	24 students	28 students	32 students
small onions	4	5	6	7	8
vegetable oil	2 oz	$2\frac{1}{2}$ oz	3 oz	$3\frac{1}{2}$ oz	4 oz
dried parsley	8 tsp	10 tsp	4 tbsp	14 tsp	16 tsp
dried basil	2 tsp	$2\frac{1}{2}$ tsp	3 tsp	$3\frac{1}{2}$ tsp	4 tsp
16-oz cans tomatoes	4 cans	5 cans	6 cans	7 cans	8 cans
6-oz cans tomato paste	4 cans	5 cans	6 cans	7 cans	8 cans
spaghetti	2 lb	$2\frac{1}{2}$ lb	3 lb	$3\frac{1}{2}$ lb	4 lb

A suggested division of responsibilities

Student A: steps 1, 2, 3
Student B: steps 4, 5, 8
Student C: steps 6, 7, 13
Student D: steps 9, 10, 11, 12

Before class

1. Provide each group with an onion.
2. Provide each group with a 16-oz can of tomatoes.
3. Provide each group with a 6-oz can of tomato paste.
4. Divide spaghetti into $\frac{1}{2}$-lb packages, providing one package for each group.

NOTES

1. Students can measure vegetable oil, water, parsley, and basil from the original containers.
2. If students would prefer a meat sauce, try adding tuna to the sauce just before serving.

Spaghetti

Makes 4 Servings

Directions

Ingredients

1 small onion

1 tbsp vegetable oil

2 tsp dried parsley

$\frac{1}{2}$ tsp dried basil

1 16-oz can tomatoes

1 6-oz can tomato paste

$\frac{1}{2}$ lb spaghetti

Utensils

paring knife

cutting board

small saucepan

wooden spoon

measuring spoons

measuring cup

can opener

large saucepan

colander

serving dish

_____ 1. Peel and chop **1 small onion**. Put in small saucepan.

_____ 2. Add **1 tbsp vegetable oil** to saucepan.

_____ 3. Cook onion, stirring frequently until it is soft.

_____ 4. Measure **2 tsp parsley** into the saucepan.

_____ 5. Measure $\frac{1}{2}$ **tsp basil** into the saucepan.

_____ 6. Add **tomatoes**. Cut large pieces of tomato into smaller pieces.

_____ 7. Add **tomato paste**.

_____ 8. Cook over medium heat 15-20 minutes until sauce thickens.

_____ 9. Put about 2 qt of water in the large saucepan. Heat water to a boil.

_____ 10. Add **spaghetti** to the boiling water.

_____ 11. Boil uncovered 8-12 minutes until tender but still firm. Stir occasionally.

_____ 12. Drain spaghetti in the colander and put in serving dish.

_____ 13. Spoon sauce over spaghetti.

Spicy Eggs and Muffins

SHOPPING LIST

(4 students per group)	16 students	20 students	24 students	28 students	32 students
vegetable-juice cocktail	24 oz	30 oz	36 oz	42 oz	48 oz
cornstarch	8 tsp	10 tsp	4 tbsp	14 tsp	16 tsp
dried marjoram	1 tsp	$1\frac{1}{4}$ tsp	$1\frac{1}{2}$ tsp	$1\frac{3}{4}$ tsp	2 tsp
turkey-ham	16 slices	20 slices	24 slices	28 slices	32 slices
English muffins	8	10	12	14	16
eggs	16	20	24	28	32

A suggested division of responsibilities

Student A: steps 1, 2, 3, 4, 5, 6, 17

Student B: steps 7, 8, 9, 10

Students C and D work together on steps 11, 12, 13, 14, 15, 16

Before class

1. Provide each group with 4 slices of turkey-ham.

2. Provide each group with 2 English muffins.

3. Provide each group with 4 eggs.

NOTES

1. Students can measure vegetable-juice cocktail, cornstarch, and marjoram from the original containers.

2. Tomato juice can be used if it is more easily available.

3. Turkey-ham is actually turkey that is ham-flavored, and is widely available. Turkey or ham slices can be substituted for turkey-ham if desired.

Spicy Eggs and Muffins

Makes 4 Servings

Directions

Ingredients

$\frac{3}{4}$ cup vegetable-juice cocktail

2 tsp cornstarch

$\frac{1}{4}$ tsp dried marjoram

4 slices turkey-ham

2 English muffins

4 eggs

Utensils

small saucepan

measuring cup

measuring spoons

wooden spoon

toaster

knife

10″ skillet

small mixing bowl

slotted spoon

_____ 1. Pour $\frac{1}{4}$ **cup vegetable-juice cocktail** into the saucepan.

_____ 2. Measure **2 tsp cornstarch** into the saucepan.

_____ 3. Mix well.

_____ 4. Add remaining $\frac{1}{2}$ cup vegetable juice to the saucepan.

_____ 5. Measure $\frac{1}{4}$ **tsp marjoram** into the saucepan.

_____ 6. Cook, stirring contantly, until sauce thickens.

_____ 7. Cut **4 slices turkey-ham** into rounds the size of the English muffins.

_____ 8. Split the **2 English muffins**.

_____ 9. Toast the muffins.

_____ 10. Place a round of turkey-ham on each toasted muffin half.

_____ 11. Put about $1\frac{1}{2}″$ water in the skillet. Heat to boiling. Reduce heat to simmer.

_____ 12. Break **egg** into small mixing bowl.

_____ 13. Gently slide egg into the water. Use spoon to shape egg as it cooks.

_____ 14. Add remaining 3 eggs to the water.

_____ 15. Cook over low heat for 3 to 5 minutes. Do not let water boil.

_____ 16. Use a slotted spoon to remove cooked eggs from the water. Place 1 egg on each muffin half.

_____ 17. Spoon sauce over eggs. Serve immediately.

Stuffed Shells

SHOPPING LIST

(4 students per group)	16 students	20 students	24 students	28 students	32 students
pasta shells	64	80	96	112	128
8-oz cans tomato sauce	4 cans	5 cans	6 cans	7 cans	8 cans
16-oz cans tomatoes	4 cans	5 cans	6 cans	7 cans	8 cans
dried oregano	4 tsp	5 tsp	6 tsp	7 tsp	8 tsp
fresh parsley	12 stems	15 stems	18 stems	21 stems	24 stems
low-fat cottage cheese	32 oz	40 oz	48 oz	56 oz	64 oz
part-skim ricotta cheese	16 oz	20 oz	24 oz	28 oz	32 oz
Parmesan cheese	$\frac{1}{2}$ cup	10 tbsp	$\frac{3}{4}$ cup	14 tbsp	1 cup
eggs	4	5	6	7	8

2 **To use this recipe in a 2-day lab**

■ On day 1, complete steps 1-17.
   Cover the shells, filling, and sauce. Refrigerate.

■ On day 2, complete steps 18-21.

A suggested division of responsibilties

Student A: steps 1, 9, 16

Student B: steps 2, 3, 4, 5

Student C: steps 6, 7, 8, 10, 11

Student D: steps 12, 13, 14, 15, 17

All students take part in steps 18, 19, 20, 21

NOTE

1. Students can measure oregano, cottage cheese, ricotta cheese, and Parmesan cheese from the original containers.

Before class

1. Provide each group with 16 shells.

2. Provide each group with 8-oz can of tomato sauce.

3. Provide each group with 16-oz can of tomatoes.

4. Provide each group with an egg.

5. Provide each group with 3 stems of fresh parsley.

Stuffed Shells

Makes 4 Servings

Directions

Ingredients

16 large pasta shells

8-oz can tomato sauce

16-oz can tomatoes

1 tsp dried oregano

1 stem fresh parsley

1 cup low-fat cottage cheese

$\frac{1}{2}$ **cup part-skim ricotta cheese**

2 tbsp Parmesan cheese

1 egg

3 stems fresh parsley

_____ 1. Preheat oven to 375°.

_____ 2. Put 3-4″ of water in kettle. Bring water to a boil.

_____ 3. Add **pasta shells** to boiling water.

_____ 4. Cook shells 10-12 minutes, stirring occasionally. Shells should be cooked, but still firm.

_____ 5. Drain shells.

_____ 6. Put **tomato sauce** in saucepan.

_____ 7. Chop **tomatoes** and add to saucepan.

_____ 8. Measure **1 tsp dried oregano** into saucepan.

_____ 9. Chop **1 stem parsley** quite fine and add to saucepan.

_____ 10. Stir and bring to a boil over medium heat.

_____ 11. Reduce heat and simmer until needed.

_____ 12. Measure **1 cup cottage cheese** into bowl.

_____ 13. Measure $\frac{1}{2}$ **cup ricotta cheese** into bowl.

_____ 14. Measure **2 tbsp Parmesan cheese** into bowl.

_____ 15. Break **egg** into bowl.

_____ 16. Chop **2 stems parsley** and add to bowl.

_____ 17. Mix cheese ingredients well.

_____ 18. Stuff cooked shells with cheese mixture.

_____ 19. Arrange stuffed shells in baking pan.

_____ 20. Pour sauce over stuffed shells.

_____ 21. Bake 20 minutes until heated through.

Utensils

kettle
saucepan
can opener
wooden spoon
measuring spoon
cutting board
paring knife
bowl
measuring cup
mixing spoon
8″ x 8″ baking pan

Stuffed Zucchini

SHOPPING LIST

(4 students per group)	16 students	20 students	24 students	28 students	32 students
zucchini	16	20	24	28	32
small onions	4	5	6	7	8
garlic	4 cloves	5 cloves	6 cloves	7 cloves	8 cloves
vegetable oil	2 oz	$2\frac{1}{2}$ oz	3 oz	$3\frac{1}{2}$ oz	4 oz
tomatoes	8	10	12	14	16
tofu	4 lb	5 lb	6 lb	7 lb	8 lb
dried parsley	4 tsp	5 tsp	6 tsp	7 tsp	8 tsp
dried basil	2 tsp	$2\frac{1}{2}$ tsp	3 tsp	$3\frac{1}{2}$ tsp	4 tsp
dried rosemary	2 tsp	$2\frac{1}{2}$ tsp	3 tsp	$3\frac{1}{2}$ tsp	4 tsp
chow mein noodles	2 cans	$2\frac{1}{2}$ cans	3 cans	$3\frac{1}{2}$ cans	4 cans
cheese	8 oz	10 oz	12 oz	14 oz	16 oz

2 **To use this recipe in a 2-day lab**
- On day 1, complete steps 1-18. Cover zucchini and refrigerate.
- On day 2, complete steps 19-23.

A suggested division of responsibilities
Student A: steps 1, 3, 12, 21
Student B: steps 2, 4, 5, 6
Student C: steps 7, 9, 10, 16
Student D: steps 8, 11, 13, 14, 15
All students take part in steps 17, 18, 19, 20, 22, 23

Before class
1. Provide each group with 4 zucchini.
2. Provide each group with an onion.
3. Provide each group with a garlic clove.
4. Provide each group with 2 tomatoes.
5. Provide each group with 1 lb tofu.
6. Divide cheese into 2-oz wedges. Give one wedge to each group.

NOTES
1. Students can measure vegetable oil, parsley, basil, and rosemary from the original containers.
2. If desired, some of the zucchini centers can be chopped up and combined with the filling.

Stuffed Zucchini

Makes 4 Servings

Directions

Ingredients
4 medium zucchini
1 small onion
1 clove garlic
1 tbsp vegetable oil
2 tomatoes
1 lb tofu
1 tsp dried parsley
$\frac{1}{2}$ tsp dried basil
$\frac{1}{2}$ tsp dried rosemary
$\frac{1}{2}$ can chow mein noodles
2 oz cheese

Utensils

kettle
slotted spoon
cutting board
paring knife
skillet
garlic press
wooden spoon
measuring spoon
baking sheet
cheese grater

_____ 1. Preheat oven to 350°.

_____ 2. Cut each **zucchini** in half the long way.

_____ 3. Half fill kettle with water and bring to a boil.

_____ 4. Put zucchini in boiling water for 5 minutes.

_____ 5. Use a slotted spoon to remove zucchini from water.

_____ 6. Scrape seeds from inside zucchini.

_____ 7. Peel **onion**. Chop onion and put in skillet.

_____ 8. Peel **garlic**. Crush and add to skillet.

_____ 9. Add **1 tbsp vegetable oil** to skillet.

_____ 10. Cook over medium heat, stirring constantly, until onion is softened.

_____ 11. Cut **tomatoes** into quarters. Remove core. Chop and add to skillet.

_____ 12. Drain **tofu**. Cut into small cubes and add to skillet.

_____ 13. Measure **1 tsp parsley** into skillet.

_____ 14. Measure $\frac{1}{2}$ **tsp basil** into skillet.

_____ 15. Measure $\frac{1}{2}$ **tsp rosemary** into skillet.

_____ 16. Stir over medium heat 2 to 3 minutes.

_____ 17. Spoon mixture into centers of zucchini.

_____ 18. Place stuffed zucchini on baking sheet.

_____ 19. Bake 15 minutes.

_____ 20. Sprinkle **chow mein noodles** over zucchini.

_____ 21. Grate **cheese**.

_____ 22. Sprinkle cheese on zucchini and return to oven.

_____ 23. When cheese melts, remove from oven and serve.

Tuna Pot Pie

SHOPPING LIST

(4 students per group)	16 students	20 students	24 students	28 students	32 students
flour	1 cup +	$1\frac{1}{4}$ cups +	$1\frac{1}{2}$ cups +	$1\frac{3}{4}$ cups +	2 cups +
whole-wheat flour	2 cups	$2\frac{1}{2}$ cups	3 cups	$3\frac{1}{2}$ cups	4 cups
margarine	1 stick	10 tbsp	$1\frac{1}{2}$ sticks	14 tbsp	2 sticks
small onions	4	5	6	7	8
dried parsley	4 tsp	5 tsp	6 tsp	7 tsp	8 tsp
chicken-flavored bouillon cubes	4	5	6	7	8
cornstarch	2 tbsp	$7\frac{1}{2}$ tsp	3 tbsp	$10\frac{1}{2}$ tsp	$\frac{1}{4}$ cup
lemons	1	$1\frac{1}{4}$	$1\frac{1}{2}$	$1\frac{3}{4}$	2
frozen peas	2 cups	$2\frac{1}{2}$ cups	3 cups	$3\frac{1}{2}$ cups	4 cups
frozen corn	2 cups	$2\frac{1}{2}$ cups	3 cups	$3\frac{1}{2}$ cups	4 cups
frozen carrots	2 cups	$2\frac{1}{2}$ cups	3 cups	$3\frac{1}{2}$ cups	4 cups
$6\frac{1}{2}$-oz cans tuna, water-packed	4 cans	5 cans	6 cans	7 cans	8 cans

2 **To use this recipe in a 2-day lab**

- On day 1, complete steps 1-21.
  Cover and refrigerate the crust and the filling.
- On day 2, complete steps 22-27.

A suggested division of responsibilities

Student A: steps 1, 4, 5, 23, 26, 27

Student B: steps 2, 3, 6, 24, 25

Student C: steps 7, 8, 9, 14, 15, 20, 21, 22

Student D: steps 10, 11, 12, 13, 16, 17, 18, 19

(continued)

Tuna Pot Pie (*continued*)

NOTES

1. Students can measure flour, water, parsley, and cornstarch from the original containers.

2. Instead of a pie, the filling can be used as a casserole. Just add a crumb topping instead of the pie crust.

3. You may have students use frozen pie crusts rather than make their own pastry.

Before class

1. Cut margarine into 2-tbsp wedges and give a wedge to each group.

2. Provide each group with an onion.

3. Provide each group with a bouillon cube.

4. Cut lemons into quarters and give each group a piece.

5. Divide peas into $\frac{1}{2}$-cup packets for each group.

6. Divide corn into $\frac{1}{2}$-cup packets for each group.

7. Divide carrots into $\frac{1}{2}$-cup packets for each group.

8. Provide each group with a can of tuna.

Tuna Pot Pie

Makes 4 Servings

Directions

Ingredients

$\frac{1}{4}$ cup all-purpose flour

$\frac{1}{2}$ cup whole-wheat flour

2 tbsp margarine

2-3 tbsp cold water

1 small onion

1 tsp parsley

$\frac{1}{2}$ cup water

1 chicken-flavored bouillon cube

$1\frac{1}{2}$ tsp cornstarch

$\frac{1}{4}$ lemon

$\frac{1}{2}$ cup frozen peas

$\frac{1}{2}$ cup frozen corn

$\frac{1}{2}$ cup frozen carrots

1 $6\frac{1}{2}$-oz can tuna, packed in water

additional flour for rolling crust

_____ 1. Preheat oven to 425°.

_____ 2. Measure $\frac{1}{4}$ cup all-purpose flour into bowl.

_____ 3. Measure $\frac{1}{2}$ cup whole-wheat flour into bowl.

_____ 4. Measure 2 tbsp margarine into bowl.

_____ 5. Use your fingers to mix margarine and flour to a coarse meal.

_____ 6. Add 2-3 tbsp cold water and mix with a fork.

_____ 7. Peel onion. Slice and put in saucepan.

_____ 8. Add 2 tbsp water to saucepan.

_____ 9. Cook over medium heat, stirring constantly, until onions are softened.

_____ 10. Measure 1 tsp parsley into saucepan.

_____ 11. Measure $\frac{1}{2}$ cup water into saucepan.

_____ 12. Add bouillon cube to saucepan.

_____ 13. Cook, stirring frequently, until bouillon cube dissolves.

_____ 14. Measure $1\frac{1}{2}$ tsp cornstarch into saucepan.

_____ 15. Cook until mixture thickens.

_____ 16. Squeeze juice of $\frac{1}{4}$ lemon into saucepan.

_____ 17. Measure $\frac{1}{2}$ cup peas into saucepan.

_____ 18. Measure $\frac{1}{2}$ cup corn into saucepan.

(continued)

Light and Tasty Cooking Labs

Tuna Pot Pie (*continued*)

Utensils

small bowl
measuring cup
fork
cutting board
paring knife
saucepan
wooden spoon
measuring spoons
can opener
rolling pin
8″ pie pan

Directions (*continued*)

_____ 19. Measure $\frac{1}{2}$ **cup carrots** into saucepan.

_____ 20. Drain **tuna**. Crumble tuna and add to saucepan.

_____ 21. Stir mixture gently.

_____ 22. Pour vegetable-fish mixture into pie pan.

_____ 23. On a lightly floured surface, roll pie crust into circle slightly larger than the pie pan.

_____ 24. Cut three 1″ slits in the center of the crust to let steam escape.

_____ 25. Put crust over the vegetable-fish mixture.

_____ 26. Pinch the edges of the crust to hold it in place.

_____ 27. Bake 20 minutes until crust browns.

Vegetable Lasagna

SHOPPING LIST

(4 students per group)	16 students	20 students	24 students	28 students	32 students
lasagna noodles	1 lb	$1\frac{1}{4}$ lb	$1\frac{1}{2}$ lb	$1\frac{3}{4}$ lb	2 lb
medium onions	4	5	6	7	8
garlic	4 cloves	5 cloves	6 cloves	7 cloves	8 cloves
mushrooms	1 lb	$1\frac{1}{4}$ lb	$1\frac{1}{2}$ lb	$1\frac{3}{4}$ lb	2 lb
broccoli	4 stalks	5 stalks	6 stalks	7 stalks	8 stalks
spinach	1 lb	$1\frac{1}{4}$ lb	$1\frac{1}{2}$ lb	$1\frac{3}{4}$ lb	2 lb
dried basil	1 tsp	$1\frac{1}{4}$ tsp	$1\frac{1}{2}$ tsp	$1\frac{3}{4}$ tsp	2 tsp
dried oregano	1 tsp	$1\frac{1}{4}$ tsp	$1\frac{1}{2}$ tsp	$1\frac{3}{4}$ tsp	2 tsp
low-fat cottage cheese	2 lb	$2\frac{1}{2}$ lb	3 lb	$3\frac{1}{2}$ lb	4 lb
part-skim mozzarella cheese	8 oz	10 oz	12 oz	14 oz	16 oz
Parmesan cheese	$\frac{1}{4}$ cup	5 tbsp	6 tbsp	7 tbsp	$\frac{1}{2}$ cup
dried parsley	4 tsp	5 tsp	6 tsp	7 tsp	8 tsp
eggs	4	5	6	7	8
black pepper	$\frac{1}{2}$ tsp	$\frac{5}{8}$ tsp	$\frac{3}{4}$ tsp	$\frac{7}{8}$ tsp	1 tsp
tomato sauce	48 oz	60 oz	72 oz	84 oz	96 oz
vegetable oil	4 oz	5 oz	6 oz	7 oz	8 oz

[2] **To use this recipe in a 2-day lab**

- On day 1, complete steps 1-22.
  Cover and refrigerate the noodles, sauce, and cheese mixture.
- On day 2, complete steps 23-30.

(continued)

Vegetable Lasagna (*continued*)

A suggested division of responsibilities

Student A: steps 1, 2, 3, 4, 5

Student B: steps 6, 8, 10, 12, 13

Student C: steps 7, 9, 11, 14, 15

Student D: steps 16, 17, 18, 19, 20, 21, 22

All students take part in steps 23, 24, 25, 26, 27, 28, 29, 30

Before class

1. Divide noodles into 4-oz packages and give a package to each group.

2. Provide each group with an onion.

3. Provide each group with a garlic clove.

4. Divide mushrooms into 4-oz packages and give a package to each group.

5. Provide each group with 1 stalk broccoli.

6. Divide spinach into $\frac{1}{4}$-lb packages and give a package to each group.

7. Provide each group with an egg.

NOTES

1. Students can measure water, basil, oregano, cottage cheese, mozzarella cheese, Parmesan cheese, parsley, black pepper, and tomato sauce from the original containers.

2. This dish can be frozen easily, then cooked at a later time.

3. If desired, you can use frozen spinach as well as canned mushrooms.

Vegetable Lasagna

Makes 4 Servings

Directions

<table>
<tr><td>Ingredients</td><td></td></tr>
</table>

Ingredients box:

4 oz lasagna noodles

1 medium onion

1 clove garlic

2 tbsp vegetable oil

4 oz mushrooms

1 stalk broccoli

$\frac{1}{4}$ lb spinach

$\frac{1}{4}$ tsp basil

$\frac{1}{4}$ tsp oregano

1 cup low-fat cottage cheese

2 oz part-skim mozzarella cheese

1 tbsp grated Parmesan cheese

1 tsp dried parsley

1 egg

$\frac{1}{8}$ tsp black pepper

$1\frac{1}{2}$ cups tomato sauce

_____ 1. Preheat oven to 375°.

_____ 2. Fill a saucepan half full of water. Cover and bring to a boil.

_____ 3. Add **lasagna noodles.** Cook uncovered 8-10 minutes until noodles are cooked, but still firm.

_____ 4. Remove noodles from hot water and place on a plate.

_____ 5. Noodles can be easily cut to fit in baking pan.

_____ 6. Peel **onion.** Slice and put in skillet.

_____ 7. Peel **garlic clove.** Crush and add to skillet.

_____ 8. Add **2 tbsp vegetable oil** to skillet. Cook, stirring constantly, until onions are softened.

_____ 9. Slice **mushrooms.** Add to skillet. Cook 2-3 minutes.

_____ 10. Chop broccoli to make about **2 cups broccoli stems & flowerets.** Add to skillet.

_____ 11. Chop spinach to make about **1 cup packed spinach.** Add to skillet.

_____ 12. Measure **$\frac{1}{4}$ tsp basil** into skillet.

_____ 13. Measure **$\frac{1}{4}$ tsp oregano** into skillet.

_____ 14. Stir to combine ingredients.

_____ 15. Cover. Reduce heat and simmer about 5 minutes until broccoli begins to cook.

(continued)

Vegetable Lasagna (*continued*)

Utensils

large saucepan with cover

wooden spoon

plate

skillet with cover

garlic press

measuring spoons

medium-size bowl

measuring cup

cheese grater

8″ x 8″ baking pan

Directions (*continued*)

_____ 16. Measure **1 cup cottage cheese** into bowl.

_____ 17. Grate **mozzarella cheese** and add to bowl.

_____ 18. Measure **2 tbsp Parmesan cheese** into bowl.

_____ 19. Measure **1 tsp parsley** into bowl.

_____ 20. Break **egg** into bowl.

_____ 21. Measure $\frac{1}{8}$ **tsp black pepper** into bowl.

_____ 22. Mix ingredients in bowl thoroughly.

_____ 23. Spread $\frac{1}{4}$ **cup of tomato sauce** in bottom of baking pan.

_____ 24. Arrange one third of the noodles on the sauce.

_____ 25. Spread half of the cheese mixture on the noodles.

_____ 26. Spread half of the vegetable mixture on the cheese.

_____ 27. Pour $\frac{1}{2}$ **cup of tomato sauce** over the vegetables.

_____ 28. Repeat steps 24-27.

_____ 29. End with a layer of noodles and the remaining $\frac{1}{4}$ cup tomato sauce.

_____ 30. Bake 20-25 minutes.

Vegetable-Tofu Casserole

SHOPPING LIST

(4 students per group)	16 students	20 students	24 students	28 students	32 students
cauliflower	1 head	$1\frac{1}{4}$ heads	$1\frac{1}{2}$ heads	$1\frac{3}{4}$ heads	2 heads
broccoli	4 stems	5 stems	6 stems	7 stems	8 stems
carrots	4	5	6	7	8
mushrooms	24	30	36	42	48
small onions	4	5	6	7	8
garlic	4 cloves	5 cloves	6 cloves	7 cloves	8 cloves
tofu	3 lb	$3\frac{3}{4}$ lb	$4\frac{1}{2}$ lb	$5\frac{1}{4}$ lb	6 lb
margarine	$\frac{1}{2}$ stick	5 tbsp	6 tbsp	7 tbsp	1 stick
flour	$\frac{1}{4}$ cup	5 tbsp	6 tbsp	7 tbsp	$\frac{1}{2}$ cup
skim milk	2 cups	$2\frac{1}{2}$ cups	3 cups	$3\frac{1}{2}$ cups	1 qt
dried basil	2 tsp	$2\frac{1}{2}$ tsp	3 tsp	$3\frac{1}{2}$ tsp	4 tsp
dried marjoram	1 tsp	$1\frac{1}{4}$ tsp	$1\frac{1}{2}$ tsp	$1\frac{3}{4}$ tsp	2 tsp
Swiss cheese	8 oz	10 oz	12 oz	14 oz	16 oz
sunflower seeds	$\frac{1}{2}$ cup	10 tbsp	$\frac{3}{4}$ cup	14 tbsp	1 cup

A suggested division of responsibilities
Student A: steps 1, 2, 4, 6, 8, 20, 21, 22
Student B: steps 3, 5, 7, 9, 23, 24
Student C: steps 10, 11, 12, 13
Student D: steps 14, 15, 16, 17, 18, 19

NOTES
1. Students can measure flour, skim milk, basil, and marjoram from the original containers.
2. Use any variety of vegetables in this recipe.
3. Instead of sunflower seeds, try crushed potato chips as a topping.

(continued)

Vegetable-Tofu Casserole (*continued*)

Before class

1. Cut cauliflower heads into quarters and give one piece to each group.

2. Provide each group with a stem of broccoli.

3. Provide a carrot for each group.

4. Provide 6 mushrooms for each group.

5. Provide each group with an onion.

6. Provide each group with a clove of garlic.

7. Divide tofu into $\frac{3}{4}$-lb chunks and give a chunk to each group.

8. Divide margarine into 1-tbsp pieces and give a piece to each group.

9. Divide cheese into 2-oz wedges and give a wedge to each group.

10. Divide sunflower seeds into 2-tbsp packets.

Vegetable-Tofu Casserole

Makes 4 Servings

Directions

Ingredients

$\frac{1}{4}$ head **cauliflower**

1 large stem **broccoli**

1 **carrot**

6 **mushrooms**

1 small **onion**

1 clove **garlic**

$\frac{3}{4}$ lb **tofu**

1 tbsp **margarine**

1 tbsp **flour**

$\frac{1}{2}$ cup **skim milk**

$\frac{1}{2}$ tsp dried **basil**

$\frac{1}{4}$ tsp dried **marjoram**

2 oz **Swiss cheese**

2 tbsp **sunflower seeds**

Utensils

cutting board
paring knife
vegetable peeler
garlic press
non-stick skillet
wooden spoon
paper towels
$\frac{1}{2}$-qt casserole dish
saucepan
measuring cup
wire whisk
measuring spoons
cheese grater

_____ 1. Preheat oven to 350°.

_____ 2. Remove core from **cauliflower**. Cut cauliflower into flowerets. Put in skillet.

_____ 3. Cut **broccoli** flowerets. Add to skillet.

_____ 4. Peel **carrot**. Cut into thin slices and add to skillet.

_____ 5. Slice **mushrooms**. Add to skillet.

_____ 6. Peel **onion**. Chop onion and add to skillet.

_____ 7. Peel **garlic**. Crush and add to skillet.

_____ 8. Add 2-3 tbsp water to skillet.

_____ 9. Cook vegetables over medium heat, stirring constantly, until vegetables are crisp-tender.

_____ 10. Wrap **tofu** with paper towels and press gently to remove excess liquid.

_____ 11. Cut tofu into $\frac{1}{2}$-inch cubes and add to vegetables.

_____ 12. Mix gently and remove from heat.

_____ 13. Put vegetable-tofu mixture in casserole dish.

_____ 14. Melt **1 tbsp margarine** in saucepan.

_____ 15. Measure **1 tbsp flour** into melted margarine and stir until smooth.

_____ 16. Gradually add $\frac{1}{2}$ **cup skim milk**, stirring constantly with a wire whisk.

_____ 17. Continue stirring and cook over medium heat until thick and bubbly.

_____ 18. Measure $\frac{1}{2}$ **tsp dried basil** into the saucepan.

_____ 19. Measure $\frac{1}{4}$ **tsp marjoram** into saucepan.

_____ 20. Grate **cheese**.

_____ 21. Add grated cheese to milk mixture and stir until cheese melts.

_____ 22. Spoon cheese sauce over the vegetable mixture.

_____ 23. Sprinkle **2 tbsp sunflower seeds** over casserole.

_____ 24. Bake 20 minutes.

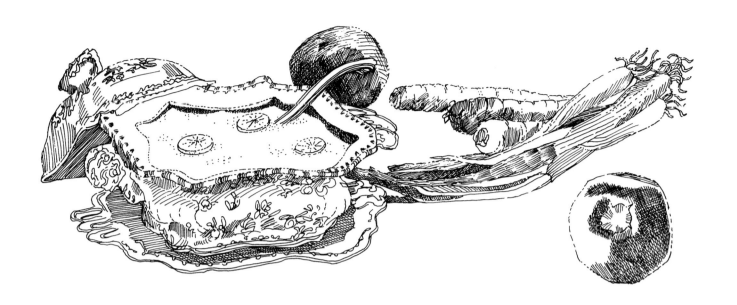

Soups

Carrot Soup

SHOPPING LIST

(4 students per group)	16 students	20 students	24 students	28 students	32 students
garlic	4 cloves	5 cloves	6 cloves	7 cloves	8 cloves
small onions	4	5	6	7	8
vegetable oil	2 oz	$2\frac{1}{2}$ oz	3 oz	$3\frac{1}{2}$ oz	4 oz
carrots	24	30	36	42	48
black pepper	$\frac{1}{2}$ tsp	$\frac{5}{8}$ tsp	$\frac{3}{4}$ tsp	$\frac{7}{8}$ tsp	1 tsp
ground cloves	$\frac{1}{2}$ tsp	$\frac{5}{8}$ tsp	$\frac{3}{4}$ tsp	$\frac{7}{8}$ tsp	1 tsp
flour	$\frac{1}{4}$ cup	5 tbsp	6 tbsp	7 tbsp	$\frac{1}{2}$ cup
chicken-flavored bouillon granules	8 tsp	10 tsp	4 tbsp	14 tsp	16 tsp

A suggested division for responsibilities

> Student A: steps 1, 3, 12, 13, 14
> Student B: steps 2, 10, 15, 16
> Student C: steps 4, 11, 17, 18
> Student D: steps 5, 6, 7, 8, 9

Before class

1. Provide each group with a garlic clove.
2. Provide each group with an onion.
3. Provide each group with 6 carrots.

NOTES

1. Students can measure vegetable oil, black pepper, cloves, water, flour, and chicken-flavored bouillon from original containers.

2. Carrot soup can be served either warm or cold.

Carrot Soup

Makes 4 Servings

Ingredients

1 clove garlic

1 small onion

1 tbsp vegetable oil

6 carrots

$\frac{1}{8}$ **tsp black pepper**

$\frac{1}{8}$ **tsp cloves**

4 cups water (divided)

1 tbsp flour

2 tsp chicken-flavored bouillon granules

Utensils

paring knife

cutting board

garlic press

saucepan with cover

wooden spoon

vegetable peeler

measuring spoons

measuring cup

blender

Directions

_____ 1. Peel **garlic**. Crush and put in saucepan.

_____ 2. Peel **onion**. Chop and put in saucepan.

_____ 3. Add **1 tbsp vegetable oil** to saucepan. Cook onion and garlic over medium heat, stirring constantly, until tender.

_____ 4. Peel **carrots**. Slice into thin slices and add to saucepan.

_____ 5. Measure $\frac{1}{8}$ **tsp black pepper** into saucepan.

_____ 6. Measure $\frac{1}{8}$ **tsp cloves** into saucepan.

_____ 7. Measure $\frac{1}{2}$ **cup water** into saucepan.

_____ 8. Stir ingredients.

_____ 9. Cover and cook over low heat 15 minutes until carrots are tender.

_____ 10. Stir in **1 tbsp flour**.

_____ 11. Measure remaining $3\frac{1}{2}$ **cups water** into saucepan.

_____ 12. Measure **2 tsp chicken-flavored bouillon granules** into saucepan.

_____ 13. Bring to a boil.

_____ 14. Simmer 5 minutes, stirring occasionally.

_____ 15. Pour mixture into blender. Depending on size of blender, this may have to be done in 2 steps.

_____ 16. Cover blender. Blend soup until smooth.

_____ 17. Return soup to saucepan and heat through.

_____ 18. Serve hot.

Chicken-Vegetable Soup

SHOPPING LIST

(4 students per group)	16 students	20 students	24 students	28 students	32 students
14-oz cans tomatoes	4 cans	5 cans	6 cans	7 cans	8 cans
carrots	16	20	24	28	32
onions	4	5	6	7	8
chicken bouillon	$\frac{1}{4}$ cup	5 tbsp	6 tbsp	7 tbsp	$\frac{1}{2}$ cup
dried thyme	4 tsp	5 tsp	6 tsp	7 tsp	8 tsp
ground sage	2 tsp	$2\frac{1}{2}$ tsp	3 tsp	$3\frac{1}{2}$ tsp	4 tsp
black pepper	1 tsp	$1\frac{1}{4}$ tsp	$1\frac{1}{2}$ tsp	$1\frac{3}{4}$ tsp	2 tsp
chicken drumsticks	16	20	24	28	32

A suggested division of responsibilities

Student A: steps 1, 4
Student B: step 2
Student C: steps 3, 5
Student D: steps 6, 7

Before class

 1. Cook chicken drumsticks. Drain. Provide 4 drumsticks for each cooking group.

2. Provide 1 can of tomatoes for each group.

3. Provide 4 carrots for each group.

4. Provide 1 onion for each group.

NOTES

1. Students can measure chicken bouillon, dried thyme, ground sage, and black pepper from the original containers.

2. This recipe can be completed as a 2-day activity. On the first day, have students in each group cook their own chicken. Chicken can be stored overnight in the refrigerator for making the soup the next day.

Chicken-Vegetable Soup

Makes 4 Servings

Ingredients

2 cups water

1 14-oz can tomatoes

4 carrots

1 large onion

1 tbsp chicken bouillon

1 tsp dried thyme

$\frac{1}{2}$ tsp ground sage

$\frac{1}{4}$ tsp black pepper

4 chicken drumsticks, cooked

Directions

_____ 1. Cut up tomatoes.

_____ 2. Wash carrot. Slice in thin slices. (No need to peel.)

_____ 3. Peel onion. Chop.

_____ 4. In saucepan, combine **2 cups water, 14-oz. can tomatoes, 4 sliced carrots, 1 chopped onion, 1 tbsp chicken bouillon, 1 tsp crushed dried thyme, $\frac{1}{2}$ tsp ground sage, and $\frac{1}{4}$ tsp black pepper.**

_____ 5. Put saucepan over heat and bring to boil. Cover and simmer for 15 minutes.

_____ 6. Remove skin from **4 chicken drumsticks**. Discard skin. Remove chicken from bones. Cut chicken into bite-sized pieces.

_____ 7. Add chicken to saucepan. Heat through.

Utensils

saucepan with cover
measuring cup
can opener
cutting board
paring knife
wooden spoon
measuring spoon

Chili
SHOPPING LIST

(4 students per group)	16 students	20 students	24 students	28 students	32 students
medium onions	4	5	6	7	8
garlic	4 cloves	5 cloves	6 cloves	7 cloves	8 cloves
vegetable oil	2 oz	$2\frac{1}{2}$ oz	3 oz	$3\frac{1}{2}$ oz	4 oz
ground turkey	2 lb	$2\frac{1}{2}$ lb	3 lb	$3\frac{1}{2}$ lb	4 lb
chili powder	8 tsp	10 tsp	4 tbsp	14 tsp	16 tsp
cumin	4 tsp	5 tsp	6 tsp	7 tsp	8 tsp
dried oregano	2 tsp	$2\frac{1}{2}$ tsp	3 tsp	$3\frac{1}{2}$ tsp	4 tsp
paprika	2 tsp	$2\frac{1}{2}$ tsp	3 tsp	$3\frac{1}{2}$ tsp	4 tsp
ground red pepper	1 tsp	$1\frac{1}{4}$ tsp	$1\frac{1}{2}$ tsp	$1\frac{3}{4}$ tsp	2 tsp
beef bouillon cubes	4	5	6	7	8
16-oz cans crushed tomatoes	4 cans	5 cans	6 cans	7 cans	8 cans
16-oz cans kidney beans	4 cans	5 cans	6 cans	7 cans	8 cans

A suggested division of responsibilities

Student A: steps 1, 5, 8

Student B: steps 2, 3, 6, 9, 10

Student C: steps 4, 7, 11

Student D: steps 12, 13, 14

NOTES

1. Students can measure vegetable oil, chili powder, cumin, oregano, paprika, and ground red pepper from the original containers.

2. It is not essential to have any meat in chili. If desired, just leave it out of this recipe.

Before class

1. Provide each group with 1 onion.

2. Provide each group with a garlic clove.

3. Divide ground turkey into $\frac{1}{2}$-lb packages and give a package to each group.

4. Provide each group with a bouillon cube.

5. Provide each group with a 16-oz can of crushed tomatoes.

6. Provide each group with a 16-oz can of kidney beans.

Chili

Makes 4 Servings

Directions

Ingredients

1 medium onion

1 garlic clove

1 tbsp vegetable oil

$\frac{1}{2}$ **lb ground turkey**

2 tsp chili powder

1 tsp cumin

$\frac{1}{2}$ **tsp oregano**

$\frac{1}{2}$ **tsp paprika**

$\frac{1}{4}$ **tsp ground
    red pepper**

1 beef bouillon cube

**1 16-oz can crushed
    tomatoes**

1 16-oz can kidney beans

_____ 1. Peel **onion** and chop. Put in saucepan.

_____ 2. Peel **garlic clove** and crush. Add to saucepan.

_____ 3. Add **1 tbsp vegetable oil**. Cook over medium heat until onions are translucent. Stir as needed.

_____ 4. Break up **turkey**. Add to saucepan.

_____ 5. Measure **2 tsp chili powder** into saucepan.

_____ 6. Measure **1 tsp cumin** into saucepan.

_____ 7. Measure $\frac{1}{2}$ **tsp oregano** into saucepan.

_____ 8. Measure $\frac{1}{2}$ **tsp paprika** into saucepan.

_____ 9. Measure $\frac{1}{4}$ **tsp ground red pepper** into saucepan.

_____ 10. Mix ingredients together.

_____ 11. Add **crushed tomatoes** to the saucepan.

_____ 12. Put water in the teakettle and bring it to a boil. Measure $\frac{1}{2}$ cup boiling water. Add **beef bouillon cube** to the water. Mix until it is dissolved. Add to the saucepan.

_____ 13. Let mixture simmer for 20 minutes.

_____ 14. Open can of **kidney beans** and add to the saucepan. Simmer 5 minutes longer.

Utensils

paring knife

cutting board

garlic press

large saucepan

measuring spoons

wooden spoon

can opener

teakettle

measuring cup

Corn Chowder

SHOPPING LIST

(4 students per group)	16 students	20 students	24 students	28 students	32 students
celery	8 stalks	10 stalks	12 stalks	14 stalks	16 stalks
green onions	12	15	18	21	24
red bell peppers	2	$2\frac{1}{2}$	3	$3\frac{1}{2}$	4
whole-kernel corn	6 cups	$7\frac{1}{2}$ cups	9 cups	$10\frac{1}{2}$ cups	12 cups
flour	$\frac{1}{2}$ cup	10 tbsp	$\frac{3}{4}$ cup	14 tbsp	1 cup
chicken-flavored bouillon granules	8 tsp	10 tsp	4 tbsp	14 tsp	16 tsp
skim milk	2 qt	$2\frac{1}{2}$ qt	3 qt	$3\frac{1}{2}$ qt	4 qt

A suggested division of responsibilities

Student A: steps 1, 4, 5

Student B: steps 2, 6

Student C: steps 3, 11, 12

Student D: steps 7, 8, 9, 10

Before class

1. Provide each group with 2 stalks of celery.

2. Provide each group with 3 green onions.

3. Cut red peppers in half and give a piece to each group.

4. Divide corn into $1\frac{1}{2}$-cup packages and give a package to each group.

NOTE

1. Students can measure water, flour, bouillon, and skim milk from the original containers.

Corn Chowder

Makes 4 Servings

Directions

Ingredients

2 stalks celery

3 green onions

$\frac{1}{2}$ red bell pepper

1 cup water

$1\frac{1}{2}$ cups whole-kernel corn

2 tbsp flour

2 tsp chicken-flavored bouillon granules

2 cups skim milk

Utensils

cutting board

paring knife

saucepan with cover

measuring cup

wooden spoon

small bowl

measuring spoon

wire whisk

_____ 1. Trim **celery**. Chop celery and put in saucepan.

_____ 2. Trim **green onions**. Chop and put in saucepan.

_____ 3. Remove seeds and stem from **red pepper**. Chop pepper and put in saucepan.

_____ 4. Measure **1 cup water** into saucepan.

_____ 5. Cover. Bring to a boil. Cook 10-15 minutes until vegetables are cooked.

_____ 6. Measure **$1\frac{1}{2}$ cups corn** into saucepan.

_____ 7. Measure **2 tbsp flour** into small bowl.

_____ 8. Measure **2 tsp chicken-flavored bouillon granules** into small bowl.

_____ 9. Gradually add **2 cups skim milk** to small bowl, using whisk to blend ingredients well.

_____ 10. Add milk mixture to saucepan.

_____ 11. Stir and heat through. Do not boil.

_____ 12. Serve hot.

Egg Drop Soup With Vegetables

SHOPPING LIST

(4 students per group)	16 students	20 students	24 students	28 students	32 students
chicken-flavored bouillon cubes	12	15	18	21	24
fresh mushrooms	16-20	20-25	24-30	28-35	32-40
frozen green peas	4 cups	5 cups	6 cups	7 cups	8 cups
eggs	8	10	12	14	16

A suggested division of responsibilities

  Student A: steps 1, 5, 6
  Student B: steps 2, 3
  Student C: steps 4, 9, 10, 11
  Student D: steps 7, 8

Before class

1. Provide each group with 3 bouillon cubes.

2. Provide each group with 4-6 mushrooms.

3. Divide frozen green peas into 1-cup packages and give a package to each group.

4. Provide each group with 2 eggs.

NOTES

1. Students can measure water directly from the faucet.

2. This is a classic Chinese soup. Using actual chicken broth will make a better-flavored soup, but chicken broth is not always available, and the bouillon is adequate.

Egg Drop Soup With Vegetables

Makes 4 Servings

Directions

Ingredients

3$\frac{1}{2}$ **cups water**

**3 chicken-flavored
bouillon cubes**

4-6 mushrooms

1 cup frozen green peas

2 eggs

Utensils

saucepan
wooden spoon
cutting board
paring knife
measuring cup
small bowl
wire whisk

_____ 1. Measure 3$\frac{1}{2}$ **cups water** into saucepan.

_____ 2. Add **bouillon cubes** to the saucepan.

_____ 3. Cook over medium heat until bouillon dissolves.

_____ 4. Slice **mushrooms**. Add to saucepan.

_____ 5. Measure **1 cup peas** and add to the saucepan.

_____ 6. Bring mixture to a boil. Boil 1 minute.

_____ 7. Break **eggs** into small bowl.

_____ 8. Use whisk to beat eggs.

_____ 9. Remove saucepan from heat.

_____ 10. Gradually add eggs to saucepan, stirring constantly, until eggs separate in strands.

_____ 11. Serve soup immediately.

Fish Soup

SHOPPING LIST

(4 students per group)	16 students	20 students	24 students	28 students	32 students
garlic	4 cloves	5 cloves	6 cloves	7 cloves	8 cloves
onions	4	5	6	7	8
celery	4 stalks	5 stalks	6 stalks	7 stalks	8 stalks
vegetable oil	2 oz	$2\frac{1}{2}$ oz	3 oz	$3\frac{1}{2}$ oz	4 oz
1-lb cans tomatoes	8 cans	10 cans	12 cans	14 cans	16 cans
dried parsley	8 tsp	10 tsp	4 tbsp	14 tsp	16 tsp
dried thyme	2 tsp	$2\frac{1}{2}$ tsp	3 tsp	$3\frac{1}{2}$ tsp	4 tsp
black pepper	4 dashes	5 dashes	6 dashes	7 dashes	8 dashes
tomato juice	16 oz	20 oz	24 oz	28 oz	32 oz
fish (fresh or frozen)	4 lb	5 lb	6 lb	7 lb	8 lb

A suggested division of responsibilities

Student A: steps 1, 6, 10, 11
Student B: steps 2, 7, 8, 9
Student C: steps 3, 4, 5, 17, 18
Student D: steps 12, 13, 14, 15, 16

Before class

1. Provide each group with a garlic clove.

2. Provide each group with an onion.

3. Provide each group with a celery stalk.

4. Provide each group with two 1-lb cans of tomatoes.

5. Provide each group with a pound of fish.

NOTE

1. Students can measure vegetable oil, parsley, thyme, black pepper, and tomato juice from the original containers.

Fish Soup

Makes 4 Servings

Directions

Ingredients

1 clove garlic

1 onion

1 celery stalk

1 tbsp vegetable oil

2 1-lb cans tomatoes

2 tsp dried parsley

$\frac{1}{2}$ tsp dried thyme

dash of black pepper

$\frac{1}{2}$ cup tomato juice

1 lb fish (fresh or frozen)

_____ 1. Peel **garlic**. Chop and put in saucepan.

_____ 2. Peel **onion**. Chop and put in saucepan.

_____ 3. Trim **celery**. Chop and put in saucepan.

_____ 4. Add **1 tbsp vegetable oil** to saucepan.

_____ 5. Cook over low heat, stirring constantly, until vegetables are softened.

_____ 6. Drain **2 cans tomatoes** and reserve juice. Chop tomatoes and add to saucepan.

_____ 7. Measure **2 tsp parsley** into saucepan.

_____ 8. Measure $\frac{1}{2}$ **tsp thyme** into saucepan.

_____ 9. Add a **dash of black pepper** to the saucepan.

_____ 10. Stir all ingredients.

_____ 11. Cover and simmer gently about 15 minutes.

_____ 12. Measure $\frac{1}{2}$ **cup tomato juice** into the second saucepan.

_____ 13. Add reserved juice from draining **tomatoes** in #6.

_____ 14. Cut **fish** into bite-sized pieces.

_____ 15. Add fish to juices.

_____ 16. Cook over low heat 8 to 10 minutes until fish is cooked.

_____ 17. Add vegetables to the fish and juice. Mix gently.

_____ 18. Serve immediately.

Utensils

cutting board

paring knife

2 saucepans with covers

wooden spoon

can opener

measuring spoons

measuring cup

Gazpacho

SHOPPING LIST

(4 students per group)	16 students	20 students	24 students	28 students	32 students
zucchini	4	5	6	7	8
green onions	8	10	12	14	16
green pepper	2	$2\frac{1}{2}$	3	$3\frac{1}{2}$	4
cucumber	4	5	6	7	8
tomatoes	8	10	12	14	16
jalapeño peppers	2	$2\frac{1}{2}$	3	$3\frac{1}{2}$	4
garlic	4 cloves	5 cloves	6 cloves	7 cloves	8 cloves
tomato juice	48 oz	60 oz	72 oz	84 oz	96 oz

A suggested division of responsibilities

Student A: steps 1, 5, 9

Student B: steps 2, 6

Student C: steps 3, 7

Student D: steps 4, 8

NOTE

1. Students can measure tomato juice from the original container.

Before class

1. Provide each group with a zucchini.

2. Provide each group with 2 green onions.

3. Cut green peppers in half and give a piece to each group.

4. Provide each group with a cucumber.

5. Provide each group with 2 tomatoes.

6. Cut jalapeño peppers in half and give a piece to each group.

7. Provide each group with a garlic clove.

Gazpacho

Makes 4 Servings

Directions

┌─────────────────────────────────┐
│ *Ingredients*   │
│   │
│ **1 small zucchini**   │
│   │
│ **2 green onions**   │
│   │
│ **$\frac{1}{2}$ green pepper**   │
│   │
│ **1 small cucumber**   │
│   │
│ **2 small tomatoes**   │
│   │
│ **$\frac{1}{2}$ jalapeño pepper**│
│   │
│ **1 clove garlic**   │
│   │
│ **$1\frac{1}{2}$ cups tomato juice** │
└─────────────────────────────────┘

_____ 1. Wash the **zucchini** and cut off the ends. Slice and put in blender.

_____ 2. Wash, trim, and chop **2 green onions**. Put in the blender.

_____ 3. Wash and remove the seeds from $\frac{1}{2}$ **green pepper**. Dice and add to blender.

_____ 4. Peel the **cucumber** and scrape off the seeds. Slice and add to the blender.

_____ 5. Wash **2 tomatoes**. Remove stems and chop. Put in the blender.

_____ 6. Remove seeds from $\frac{1}{2}$ **jalapeño pepper**. Wash and chop into very fine pieces. Put in blender.

_____ 7. Peel **garlic clove**. Mince in garlic press and add to blender.

_____ 8. Measure $1\frac{1}{2}$ **cups tomato juice** into the blender.

_____ 9. Put cover on blender and blend for a few seconds to mix and chop vegetables. Soup should be chunky. Served chilled.

Utensils

cutting board
paring knife
blender
garlic press
measuring cup

Meatball Stew

SHOPPING LIST

(4 students per group)	16 students	20 students	24 students	28 students	32 students
ground beef	2 lb	$2\frac{1}{2}$ lb	3 lb	$3\frac{1}{2}$ lb	4 lb
bread crumbs	1 cup	$1\frac{1}{4}$ cups	$1\frac{1}{2}$ cups	$1\frac{3}{4}$ cups	2 cups
Worcestershire sauce	2 tbsp	$7\frac{1}{2}$ tsp	3 tbsp	$10\frac{1}{2}$ tsp	4 tbsp
black pepper	4 dashes	5 dashes	6 dashes	7 dashes	8 dashes
small onions	4	5	6	7	8
carrots	8	10	12	14	16
potatoes	4	5	6	7	8
8-oz cans tomato sauce	4 cans	5 cans	6 cans	7 cans	8 cans
8-oz cans peas	4 cans	5 cans	6 cans	7 cans	8 cans

A suggested division of responsibilities

Student A: steps 1, 3, 5, 6 (with B)
Student B: steps 2, 4, 6 (with A), 7
Student C: steps 8, 9, 13, 14
Student D: steps 10, 11, 12, 15

NOTE

1. Students can measure Worcestershire sauce, black pepper, and water from their original containers.

Before class

1. Divide ground beef into $\frac{1}{2}$-lb packages and give a package to each group.

2. Measure dry bread crumbs into $\frac{1}{4}$-cup packages and give a package to each group.

3. Provide each group with an onion.

4. Provide each group with 2 carrots.

5. Provide each group with a potato.

6. Provide each group with an 8-oz can of tomato sauce.

7. Provide each group with an 8-oz can of peas.

Meatball Stew

Makes 4 Servings

Directions

Ingredients

$\frac{1}{2}$ **lb ground beef**

$\frac{1}{4}$ **cup fine dry bread crumbs**

$1\frac{1}{2}$ **tsp Worcestershire sauce**

black pepper

1 small onion

2 carrots

1 potato

1 8-oz can tomato sauce

1 cup water

1 8-oz can peas

_____ 1. Put **ground beef** in small bowl.

_____ 2. Measure $\frac{1}{4}$ **cup bread crumbs** into bowl.

_____ 3. Measure $1\frac{1}{2}$ **tsp Worcestershire sauce** into bowl.

_____ 4. Sprinkle with **black pepper**.

_____ 5. Mix ingredients well.

_____ 6. Shape into 12 small meatballs and place in skillet.

_____ 7. Brown meatballs over medium heat. Stir frequently to brown all sides.

_____ 8. Peel and slice **onion**. Add to saucepan.

_____ 9. Peel and slice **2 carrots**. Add to saucepan.

_____ 10. Peel and dice **potato**. Add to saucepan.

_____ 11. Add **tomato sauce** to saucepan.

_____ 12. Add **water** to saucepan.

_____ 13. Stir. Bring to a boil. Reduce heat. Cover and simmer 20 minutes until vegetables are tender.

_____ 14. Add **peas**.

_____ 15. Add meatballs. Warm through.

Utensils

small bowl

measuring cup

measuring spoons

wooden spoon

skillet

saucepan with cover

cutting board

vegetable peeler

paring knife

can opener

Mexican Soup

SHOPPING LIST

(4 students per group)	16 students	20 students	24 students	28 students	32 students
small onions	4	5	6	7	8
vegetable oil	2 oz	$2\frac{1}{2}$ oz	3 oz	$3\frac{1}{2}$ oz	4 oz
chicken-flavored bouillon cubes	8	10	12	14	16
small zucchini	8	10	12	14	16
8-oz cans whole-kernel corn	4 cans	5 cans	6 cans	7 cans	8 cans
green chili peppers	4–8	5–10	6–12	7–14	8–16
skim milk	1 qt	5 cups	$1\frac{1}{2}$ qt	7 cups	2 qt
cheddar cheese	8 oz	10 oz	12 oz	14 oz	16 oz
fresh parsley	8 stems	10 stems	12 stems	14 stems	16 stems
ground nutmeg	2 tsp	$2\frac{1}{2}$ tsp	3 tsp	$3\frac{1}{2}$ tsp	4 tsp

A suggested division of responsibilities

    Student A: steps 1, 4, 12

    Student B: steps 2, 3, 5, 13

    Student C: steps 6, 9, 10, 14

    Student D: steps 7, 8, 11

    All students take part in step 15

NOTE

    1. Students can measure vegetable oil, water, milk, and nutmeg from original containers.

Before class

1. Provide each group with an onion.

2. Provide each group with 2 bouillon cubes.

3. Provide each group with 2 zucchini.

4. Provide each group with an 8-oz can of whole-kernel corn.

5. Provide each group with 1 or 2 green chili peppers.

6. Divide cheese into 2-oz wedges and give a wedge to each group.

7. Provide each group with 2 stems fresh parsley.

Mexican Soup

Makes 4 Servings

Directions

_____	1. Peel **onion**. Slice and put in the saucepan.
_____	2. Add **1 tbsp vegetable oil** to the saucepan.
_____	3. Cook over medium heat, stirring constantly, until onion is softened.
_____	4. Measure **2 cups water** into the saucepan.
_____	5. Add **2 chicken bouillon cubes**. Stir over medium heat until bouillon cubes dissolve.
_____	6. Trim ends from **zucchini**. Dice unpeeled zucchini and add to the saucepan.
_____	7. Drain liquid from **corn**. Add corn to saucepan.
_____	8. Chop chili peppers very finely. Add **2 tbsp chili peppers** to the saucepan.
_____	9. Bring the soup to a boil.
_____	10. Cover pan and cook over medium heat about 5 minutes until zucchini is tender.
_____	11. Measure **1 cup skim milk** into the saucepan. Heat through.
_____	12. Grate cheese while soup is cooking.
_____	13. Chop parsley.
_____	14. Ladle soup into bowls.
_____	15. Garnish each bowl with grated **cheese**, chopped **parsley**, and **nutmeg**.

Ingredients

1 small onion

1 tbsp vegetable oil

2 cups water

2 chicken-flavored bouillon cubes

2 small zucchini

1 8-oz can whole-kernel corn

1 or 2 green chili peppers (fresh or canned)

1 cup skim milk

2 oz cheddar cheese

2 stems fresh parsley

$\frac{1}{2}$ tsp nutmeg

Utensils

large saucepan with cover

paring knife

cutting board

wooden spoon

can opener

measuring cup

measuring spoons

cheese grater

Peanut Butter-Vegetable Soup
SHOPPING LIST

(4 students per group)	16 students	20 students	24 students	28 students	32 students
chicken-flavored bouillon cubes	8	10	12	14	16
large potatoes	8	10	12	14	16
carrots	12	15	18	21	24
celery	4 stalks	5 stalks	6 stalks	7 stalks	8 stalks
small onions	4	5	6	7	8
garlic	4 cloves	5 cloves	6 cloves	7 cloves	8 cloves
small zucchini	4	5	6	7	8
broccoli	4 stems	5 stems	6 stems	7 stems	8 stems
tomatoes	4	5	6	7	8
peanut butter (smooth)	1 cup	$1\frac{1}{4}$ cups	$1\frac{1}{2}$ cups	$1\frac{3}{4}$ cups	2 cups
black pepper	1 tsp	$1\frac{1}{4}$ tsp	$1\frac{1}{2}$ tsp	$1\frac{3}{4}$ tsp	2 tsp
dried parsley	2 tsp	$2\frac{1}{2}$ tsp	3 tsp	$3\frac{1}{2}$ tsp	4 tsp

A suggested division of responsibilities

    Student A: steps 1, 2, 7, 13
    Student B: steps 3, 8, 9, 14
    Student C: steps 4, 10, 15, 16, 17
    Student D: steps 5, 6, 11, 12

NOTES

1. Students can measure water, peanut butter, black pepper, and parsley from the original containers.
2. Any variety of vegetables can be used in this recipe in addition to the vegetables listed or to replace some not available.

Before class

1. Provide each group with 2 bouillon cubes.
2. Provide each group with 2 potatoes.
3. Provide each group with 3 carrots.
4. Provide each group with 1 celery stalk.
5. Provide each group with an onion.
6. Provide each group with a garlic clove.
7. Provide each group with a zucchini.
8. Provide each group with a stem of broccoli.
9. Provide each group with a tomato.

Peanut Butter-Vegetable Soup

Makes 4 Servings

Ingredients

4 cups water

2 chicken-flavored
bouillon cubes

2 large potatoes

3 carrots

1 stalk celery

1 small onion

1 clove garlic

1 small zucchini

1 small stem broccoli

1 tomato

$\frac{1}{4}$ cup natural smooth
peanut butter
(no sugar added)

$\frac{1}{4}$ tsp black pepper

$\frac{1}{2}$ tsp dried parsley

Utensils

large saucepan with cover
paring knife
cutting board
vegetable peeler
wooden spoon
garlic press
measuring cup
measuring spoons

Directions

_____ 1. Measure **4 cups water** into saucepan. Cover and bring to a boil.

_____ 2. Add **2 bouillon cubes**. Stir until dissolved.

_____ 3. Peel **potatoes**. Cut into cubes. Add to pot.

_____ 4. Peel **carrots**. Slice. Add to pot.

_____ 5. Trim **celery stalk**. Slice and add to pot.

_____ 6. Peel **onion**. Slice and add to pot.

_____ 7. Peel **garlic clove**. Crush and add to pot.

_____ 8. Bring soup to a boil. Cover and cook over medium heat about 10 minutes until vegetables begin to cook.

_____ 9. Remove stem ends from **zucchini**. Slice and add to pot.

_____ 10. Cut flowerets from **broccoli** stem and add to pot.

_____ 11. Cut **tomato** into quarters. Remove core. Chop tomato and add to pot.

_____ 12. Simmer the soup about 8 minutes until vegetables cook.

_____ 13. Measure $\frac{1}{4}$ **cup smooth peanut butter** into the pot.

_____ 14. Measure $\frac{1}{4}$ **tsp black pepper** into the pot.

_____ 15. Measure $\frac{1}{2}$ **tsp parsley** into the pot.

_____ 16. Stir soup until the peanut butter is fully blended.

_____ 17. Heat through and serve.

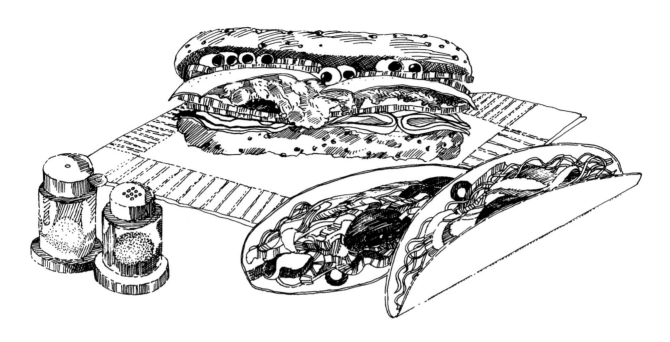

Sandwiches

Apple-Tuna Toasts

SHOPPING LIST

(4 students per group)	16 students	20 students	24 students	28 students	32 students
$6\frac{1}{2}$-oz cans tuna (water-packed)	4 cans	5 cans	6 cans	7 cans	8 cans
apples	2	$2\frac{1}{2}$	3	$3\frac{1}{2}$	4
celery	2 stalks	$2\frac{1}{2}$ stalks	3 stalks	$3\frac{1}{2}$ stalks	4 stalks
reduced-calorie mayonniase	4 oz	5 oz	6 oz	7 oz	8 oz
black pepper	4 dashes	5 dashes	6 dashes	7 dashes	8 dashes
raisin bread	16 slices	20 slices	24 slices	28 slices	32 slices

A suggested division of responsibilities

    Student A: steps 1, 2, 5

    Student B: steps 3, 6

    Student C: steps 4, 7

    Student D: steps 8, 9

    All students take part in step 10

NOTES

1. Students can measure mayonnaise and black pepper from original containers.

2. You may want to have students make *Irish Soda Bread* (with raisins) on page 170 to use in this recipe.

Before class

1. Provide a can of tuna for each group.

2. Cut the apples in half and give half an apple to each group.

3. Cut celery stalks in half and give half a stalk of celery to each group.

4. Provide 4 slices of raisin bread for each group.

Apple-Tuna Toasts

Makes 4 Servings

Directions

Ingredients

1 $6\frac{1}{2}$-oz can tuna
   packed in water

$\frac{1}{2}$ apple

$\frac{1}{2}$ stalk celery

2 tbsp reduced-calorie
   mayonnaise

dash of pepper

4 slices raisin bread

Utensils

can opener
small bowl
fork
cutting board
paring knife
measuring spoons
toaster

_____ 1. Open **can of tuna**. Drain liquid. Put tuna in bowl.

_____ 2. Use a fork to flake the tuna.

_____ 3. Cut $\frac{1}{2}$ **apple** in half. Remove core. Chop apple into fine pieces. Add to bowl.

_____ 4. Wash $\frac{1}{2}$ **stalk celery**. Chop into fine pieces and add to bowl.

_____ 5. Measure **2 tbsp mayonnaise** into bowl.

_____ 6. Sprinkle with **black pepper**.

_____ 7. Mix well.

_____ 8. Toast the **raisin bread**.

_____ 9. Divide the tuna mixture among the four slices of toast.

_____ 10. Spread the tuna to cover the toast.

Beefwiches

SHOPPING LIST

(4 students per group)	16 students	20 students	24 students	28 students	32 students
lean ground beef	2 lb	$2\frac{1}{2}$ lb	3 lb	$3\frac{1}{2}$ lb	4 lb
green pepper	1	$1\frac{1}{4}$	$1\frac{1}{2}$	$1\frac{3}{4}$	2
garlic	4 cloves	5 cloves	6 cloves	7 cloves	8 cloves
flour	4 tsp	5 tsp	6 tsp	7 tsp	8 tsp
plain low-fat yogurt	16 oz	20 oz	24 oz	28 oz	32 oz
Worcestershire sauce	2 tsp	$2\frac{1}{2}$ tsp	3 tsp	$3\frac{1}{2}$ tsp	4 tsp
black pepper	4 dashes	5 dashes	6 dashes	7 dashes	8 dashes
French rolls	8	10	12	14	16
medium tomatoes	4	5	6	7	8
part-skim mozzarella cheese	8 oz	10 oz	12 oz	14 oz	16 oz

A suggested division of responsibilities

Student A: steps 2, 4, 6, 17

Student B: steps 3, 5, 7, 18, 19

Student C: steps 8, 9, 10, 11, 12, 16

Student D: steps 1, 13, 14, 15, 20

NOTES

1. Students can measure flour, yogurt, Worcestershire sauce, and black pepper from original containers.

2. If French rolls are not available, use slices of French bread.

Before class

1. Divide lean ground beef into $\frac{1}{2}$-lb packages and give a package to each group.

2. Cut green pepper in quarters and give each group a piece.

3. Provide each group with a garlic clove.

4. Provide each group with 2 French rolls.

5. Provide each group with a medium tomato.

6. Divide cheese into 2-oz wedges and give a wedge to each group.

Beefwiches

Makes 4 Servings

Directions

Ingredients

$\frac{1}{2}$ **lb lean ground beef**

$\frac{1}{4}$ **green pepper**

1 clove garlic

1 tsp flour

$\frac{1}{2}$ **cup plain low-fat yogurt**

$\frac{1}{2}$ **tsp Worcestershire sauce**

dash black pepper

2 French rolls

1 medium tomato

2 oz part-skim mozzarella cheese

Utensils

skillet

sharp knife

chopping board

wooden spoon

measuring spoons

measuring cup

small sauce dish

broiling pan

cheese grater

_____ 1. Preheat oven to broil.

_____ 2. Break up $\frac{1}{2}$ **lb ground beef** and put in skillet.

_____ 3. Remove stem and seeds from **green pepper**. Chop green pepper and put in skillet.

_____ 4. Peel **garlic**. Chop garlic into very fine pieces and add to skillet.

_____ 5. Heat skillet over medium heat. Cook beef, pepper, and garlic, stirring occasionally until beef is browned.

_____ 6. Drain fat.

_____ 7. Sprinkle **flour** over hamburg mixture and stir in.

_____ 8. Measure $\frac{1}{2}$ **cup yogurt** into small sauce dish.

_____ 9. Measure $\frac{1}{2}$ **tsp Worcestershire sauce** into small sauce dish.

_____ 10. Sprinkle **dash of black pepper** in sauce dish.

_____ 11. Mix ingredients in sauce dish and add to skillet.

_____ 12. Heat mixture, but do not boil.

_____ 13. Slice **rolls** in half lengthwise.

_____ 14. Place rolls cut-side up on broiling pan.

_____ 15. Broil rolls about 2 minutes until toasted.

_____ 16. Spread one-quarter of meat mixture on each piece of roll.

_____ 17. Slice **tomato** and put a tomato slice on each sandwich.

_____ 18. Grate **cheese** while meat is cooking.

_____ 19. Sprinkle grated cheese on each sandwich.

_____ 20. Broil about 2 minutes until cheese melts.

Chicken Tacos

SHOPPING LIST

(4 students per group)	16 students	20 students	24 students	28 students	32 students
taco shells	16	20	24	28	32
vegetable oil	2 oz	$2\frac{1}{2}$ oz	3 oz	$3\frac{1}{2}$ oz	4 oz
onions (medium)	4	5	6	7	8
garlic cloves	12	15	18	21	24
tomatoes (large)	4	5	6	7	8
8 oz cans tomato sauce	4 cans	5 cans	6 cans	7 cans	8 cans
hot sauce	4 dashes	5 dashes	6 dashes	7 dashes	8 dashes
oregano leaves	2 tsp	$2\frac{1}{2}$ tsp	3 tsp	$3\frac{1}{2}$ tsp	4 tsp
chicken drumsticks	12	15	18	21	24
cheddar cheese	8 oz	10 oz	12 oz	14 oz	16 oz
lettuce (small heads)	1	$1\frac{1}{4}$	$1\frac{1}{2}$	$1\frac{3}{4}$	2

A suggested division of responsibilities

Student A: steps 1, 6

Student B: steps 2, 3, 4, 5, 7

Student C: step 8

Student D: steps 9, 10

All students take part in steps 11, 12

NOTES

1. Students can measure vegetable oil, hot sauce, and oregano leaves directly from the original containers.

2. Any cooked chicken can be used in this recipe—drumsticks are suggested because they are easy to divide and relatively inexpensive.

Before class

 1. Cook chicken drumsticks. Drain. Provide 3 drumsticks for each group.

2. Provide 4 taco shells for each group.

3. Provide 1 onion for each group.

4. Provide 3 garlic cloves for each group.

5. Provide a tomato for each group.

6. Divide cheese into 2-oz blocks.

7. Divide heads of lettuce into quarters.

8. Provide an 8-oz can of tomato sauce for each group.

Chicken Tacos

Makes 4 Servings

Directions

<table>
<tr><td rowspan="12">Ingredients

4 taco shells

1 tbsp vegetable oil

1 medium onion

3 garlic cloves

1 large tomato

1 8-oz can tomato sauce

dash of hot sauce

$\frac{1}{2}$ tsp oregano leaves

3 chicken drumsticks (cooked)

2 oz cheddar cheese

$\frac{1}{4}$ small head of lettuce</td></tr>
</table>

_____ 1. Preheat oven to 300°. Place **4 taco shells** on baking sheet and heat in oven about 5 minutes.

_____ 2. Peel **1 medium onion**. Chop.

_____ 3. Peel **3 garlic cloves**. Put through garlic press.

_____ 4. Heat **1 tbsp vegetable oil** in skillet.

_____ 5. Add onion and garlic. Sauté until onion is translucent (about 5 minutes).

_____ 6. Chop **1 large tomato** into small pieces.

_____ 7. Add to skillet: Chopped tomato, **8-oz can tomato sauce, a dash of hot sauce**, and $\frac{1}{2}$ **tsp oregano leaves**. Cook about 5 minutes. Stir occasionally.

_____ 8. Remove skin from **3 chicken drumsticks**. Discard skin. Remove chicken from bones. Cut chicken into bite-sized pieces. Add chicken to skillet. Heat through.

_____ 9. Grate **2 oz cheddar cheese**.

_____ 10. Shred $\frac{1}{4}$ **small head of lettuce**.

_____ 11. Divide chicken mixture into taco shells.

_____ 12. Top each taco with shredded cheese and lettuce.

Utensils

baking sheet

skillet

measuring spoons

garlic press

cutting board

paring knife

wooden spoon

can opener

cheese grater

Greek-Style Pita Burgers

SHOPPING LIST

(4 students per group)	16 students	20 students	24 students	28 students	32 students
firm tofu	1 lb	$1\frac{1}{4}$ lb	$1\frac{1}{2}$ lb	$1\frac{3}{4}$ lb	2 lb
ground beef	2 lb	$2\frac{1}{2}$ lb	3 lb	$3\frac{1}{2}$ lb	4 lb
soy sauce	4 tsp	5 tsp	6 tsp	7 tsp	8 tsp
tahini dip & dressing mix	4 tsp	5 tsp	6 tsp	7 tsp	8 tsp
cornstarch	4 tsp	5 tsp	6 tsp	7 tsp	8 tsp
mung bean sprouts	4 cups	5 cups	6 cups	7 cups	8 cups
4″ pita rounds	16	20	24	28	32

A suggested division of responsibilities

Student A: steps 1, 2, 6, 7
Student B: steps 3, 4, 5, 13
Student C: steps 8, 9, 10, 11, 12
Student D: steps 14, 15

Before class

1. Divide tofu into $\frac{1}{4}$-lb chunks and give one to each group.

2. Divide ground beef into $\frac{1}{2}$-lb packages and give one to each group.

3. Provide each group with 1 cup mung bean sprouts.

4. Provide each group with 4 pita rounds.

NOTES

1. Students can measure soy sauce, water, tahini dip, and cornstarch from original containers.

2. Tahini dip & dressing mix is available in the gourmet section of the supermarket.

Greek-Style Pita Burgers

Makes 4 Servings

Directions

Ingredients

$\frac{1}{4}$ **lb firm tofu**

$\frac{1}{2}$ **lb lean ground beef**

1 tsp soy sauce

$\frac{1}{4}$ **cup water**

**1 tsp tahini dip
and dressing mix**

1 tsp cornstarch

1 cup mung bean sprouts

4 4″ pita rounds

Utensils

bowl

fork

measuring spoons

non-stick skillet

wooden spoon

small dish

sharp knife

_____ 1. Rinse **tofu** in cold water. Drain and blot dry. Put in bowl.

_____ 2. Use a fork to flake the tofu.

_____ 3. Add $\frac{1}{2}$ **lb ground beef** to the bowl.

_____ 4. Measure **1 tsp soy sauce** into the bowl.

_____ 5. Blend tofu, ground beef, and soy sauce together.

_____ 6. Spoon meat mixture into the skillet.

_____ 7. Cook over medium heat, stirring frequently, until beef is lightly browned.

_____ 8. Measure $\frac{1}{4}$ **cup water** into small dish.

_____ 9. Measure **1 tsp tahini dip & dressing mix** into dish.

_____ 10. Measure **1 tsp cornstarch** into small dish.

_____ 11. Mix the ingredients in the dish and add to the skillet.

_____ 12. Stir and cook until the mixture is slightly thickened.

_____ 13. Stir in **bean sprouts** and heat through.

_____ 14. Cut **4 pita rounds** open along edge.

_____ 15. Spoon beef mixture into the pita round.

Huevos Rancheros

SHOPPING LIST

(4 students per group)	16 students	20 students	24 students	28 students	32 students
curly lettuce leaves	16	20	24	28	32
6″ corn tortillas	16	20	24	28	32
small onions	4	5	6	7	8
green peppers	2	$2\frac{1}{2}$	3	$3\frac{1}{2}$	4
vegetable oil	4 oz	5 oz	6 oz	7 oz	8 oz
chili peppers (fresh or canned)	8	10	12	14	16
tomatoes	4	5	6	7	8
eggs	16	20	24	28	32
black pepper	4 dashes	5 dashes	6 dashes	7 dashes	8 dashes
hot sauce	8-10 dashes	10-15 dashes	12-18 dashes	14-21 dashes	16-24 dashes
cheddar cheese	8 oz	10 oz	12 oz	14 oz	16 oz
chili powder	4 sprinkles	5 sprinkles	6 sprinkles	7 sprinkles	8 sprinkles

A suggested division of responsibilities

Student A: steps 1, 2, 3, 4, 5, 6, 23
Student B: steps 7, 9, 10, 14
Student C: steps 8, 11, 12, 13
Student D: steps 15, 16, 17, 18, 19, 20, 21, 22
All students take part in steps 24, 25

NOTES

1. Students can measure black pepper, hot sauce, vegetable oil, and chili powder directly from original containers.

2. If preferred, use boxed tortillas; this may eliminate the need for some preparation steps.

Before class

1. Provide 4 curly lettuce leaves for each group.
2. Provide 4 corn tortillas for each group.
3. Provide a small onion for each group.
4. Cut green peppers in half and give a piece to each group.
5. Provide 2 chili peppers for each group.
6. Provide a tomato for each group.
7. Provide 4 eggs for each group.
8. Cut cheese into 2-oz wedges and give a wedge to each group.

Huevos Rancheros

Makes 4 Servings

Directions

<table>
<tr><td></td><td>Ingredients</td></tr>
</table>

Ingredients

4 large curly lettuce leaves

4 6″ corn tortillas

1 small onion

$\frac{1}{2}$ **green pepper**

2 tbsp vegetable oil (divided)

2 green chili peppers (fresh or canned)

1 tomato

4 eggs

dash black pepper

2 or 3 dashes hot sauce

2 oz cheddar cheese

sprinkle of chili powder

Directions

_____ 1. Preheat oven to broil.

_____ 2. Arrange **lettuce leaves** on each plate.

_____ 3. Place **4 tortillas** on broiler pan.

_____ 4. Broil tortillas 1 or 2 minutes until light brown.

_____ 5. Turn tortillas and brown second side.

_____ 6. Place a tortilla on each lettuce bed.

_____ 7. Peel **onion**. Chop onion and put in skillet.

_____ 8. Remove seeds and stem from **green pepper**. Chop green pepper and add to skillet.

_____ 9. Add **1 tbsp vegetable oil** to skillet.

_____ 10. Cook vegetables over medium heat until softened, stirring constantly.

_____ 11. Chop **green chili peppers** and add to skillet.

_____ 12. Cut **tomato** in quarters. Remove stem. Chop tomato and add to skillet.

_____ 13. Cook, stirring constantly, until tomatoes and chili peppers are heated through.

_____ 14. Spoon vegetable mixture over hot tortillas.

_____ 15. Break **eggs** into small bowl.

_____ 16. Add a **dash of black pepper** to the eggs.

_____ 17. Add **2-3 dashes of hot sauce** to the eggs.

_____ 18. Use a fork to mix the ingredients in the small bowl.

_____ 19. Measure **1 tbsp vegetable oil** into heated skillet, tipping skillet to be sure oil coats entire pan lightly.

_____ 20. Add eggs to skillet.

_____ 21. Cook over medium heat, stirring until slightly scrambled.

_____ 22. Spoon scrambled egg over each tortilla with vegetables.

_____ 23. Grate **cheese** while vegetables are heating.

_____ 24. Sprinkle grated cheese on the eggs.

_____ 25. Top each serving with **a dash of chili powder.**

Utensils

4 luncheon plates
broiling pan
cutting board
paring knife
non-stick skillet
wooden spoon
measuring spoons
small bowl
fork
cheese grater

Pita Heroes

SHOPPING LIST

(4 students per group)	16 students	20 students	24 students	28 students	32 students
6″ pitas (whole wheat)	8	10	12	14	16
turkey-ham	16 slices	20 slices	24 slices	28 slices	32 slices
low-fat cheese	16 slices	20 slices	24 slices	28 slices	32 slices
lettuce	$\frac{1}{2}$ head	$\frac{5}{8}$ head	$\frac{3}{4}$ head	$\frac{7}{8}$ head	1 head
tomatoes	4	5	6	7	8
green peppers	4	5	6	7	8
dill pickle slices	64-80	80-100	96-120	112-140	128-160
small onions	4	5	6	7	8
reduced-calorie Italian dressing	8 oz	10 oz	12 oz	14 oz	16 oz

A suggested division of responsibilities

    Student A: steps 1, 5

    Student B: steps 2, 6

    Student C: steps 3, 8

    Student D: steps 4, 7

    All students take part in step 9

NOTES

1. Students can measure dressing from original container.

2. Turkey-ham is actually turkey that is ham-flavored; it is widely available. If desired, turkey or ham slices can be substituted.

Before class

1. Provide each group with 2 pita rounds.

2. Provide each group with 4 slices of turkey-ham.

3. Provide each group with 4 slices of low-fat cheese.

4. Cut head of lettuce into eighths and give a piece to each group.

5. Provide each group with a tomato.

6. Provide each group with a green pepper.

7. Provide each group with 16-20 dill pickle slices.

8. Provide each group with an onion.

Pita Heroes

Makes 4 Servings

Directions

Ingredients

2 6″ whole-wheat pita
   rounds

4 slices turkey-ham

4 slices low-fat cheese

$\frac{1}{8}$ head lettuce

1 large tomato

1 small green pepper

16-20 dill pickle slices

1 small onion

$\frac{1}{4}$ cup reduced-calorie
   Italian dressing

_____ 1. Cut **2 pita rounds** in half to make 4 pockets.

_____ 2. Put 1 slice **turkey-ham** in each pocket.

_____ 3. Put 1 slice **cheese** in each pocket.

_____ 4. Shred **lettuce**. Divide lettuce among 4 sandwiches.

_____ 5. Cut **tomato** into quarters. Remove core. Slice $\frac{1}{4}$ tomato into each sandwich.

_____ 6. Cut **green pepper** into quarters. Remove seeds and stem. Slice $\frac{1}{4}$ green pepper into each sandwich.

_____ 7. Put 4 or 5 **dill pickle slices** in each sandwich.

_____ 8. Peel **onion**. Slice. Divide onion among 4 sandwiches.

_____ 9. Top each sandwich with 1 tbsp **Italian dressing**.

Utensils

sharp knife
cutting board
measuring spoons

Pita Pizzas

SHOPPING LIST

(4 students per group)	16 students	20 students	24 students	28 students	32 students
6″ pitas (whole wheat)	8	10	12	14	16
pizza sauce	16 oz	20 oz	24 oz	28 oz	32 oz
chicken franks	8	10	12	14	16
green peppers	2	$2\frac{1}{2}$	3	$3\frac{1}{2}$	4
part-skim mozzarella cheese	8 oz	10 oz	12 oz	14 oz	16 oz

A suggested division of responsibilities

Student A: steps 1, 6
Student B: steps 2, 4
Student C: steps 3, 7
Student D: steps 5, 8

NOTE

1. Students can measure pizza sauce from original container.

Before class

1. Provide each group with 2 pita rounds.

2. Provide each group with 2 chicken franks.

3. Cut each green pepper in half and give a piece to each group.

4. Cut cheese into 2-oz wedges and give a wedge to each group.

Pita Pizzas

Makes 4 Servings

Directions

_____	1.	Preheat oven to broil.

Ingredients

2 6″ whole-wheat pita rounds

$\frac{1}{2}$ **cup pizza sauce**

2 chicken franks

$\frac{1}{2}$ **green pepper**

2 oz part-skim mozzarella cheese

_____ 1. Preheat oven to broil.

_____ 2. Split **2 whole-wheat pitas** to make 4 rounds.

_____ 3. Place pitas on baking sheet, smooth side down.

_____ 4. Spread **pizza sauce** on each piece of pita.

_____ 5. Slice **chicken franks**. Arrange slices on the 4 pizzas.

_____ 6. Remove seeds from **green pepper**. Chop green pepper. Divide chopped green pepper among 4 pizzas.

_____ 7. Grate **cheese**. Sprinkle grated cheese on each pizza.

_____ 8. Broil pizzas 3-5 minutes until cheese melts and the pizzas are heated through.

Utensils

sharp knife

cutting board

spoon

cheese grater

baking sheet

Tostadas

SHOPPING LIST

(4 students per group)	16 students	20 students	24 students	28 students	32 students
6″ flour tortillas	16	20	24	28	32
garlic	4 cloves	5 cloves	6 cloves	7 cloves	8 cloves
small onions	4	5	6	7	8
jalapeno peppers	4	5	6	7	8
vegetable oil	2 oz	$2\frac{1}{2}$ oz	3 oz	$3\frac{1}{2}$ oz	4 oz
ground turkey	2 lb	$2\frac{1}{2}$ lb	3 lb	$3\frac{1}{2}$ lb	4 lb
tomato sauce	24 oz	30 oz	36 oz	42 oz	48 oz
dried oregano	3 tsp	$3\frac{3}{4}$ tsp	$4\frac{1}{2}$ tsp	$5\frac{1}{4}$ tsp	6 tsp
dried thyme	1 tsp	$1\frac{1}{4}$ tsp	$1\frac{1}{2}$ tsp	$1\frac{3}{4}$ tsp	2 tsp
hot sauce	4 dashes	5 dashes	6 dashes	7 dashes	8 dashes
part-skim mozzarella cheese	4 oz	5 oz	6 oz	7 oz	8 oz
reduced-calorie sour cream	8 oz	10 oz	12 oz	14 oz	16 oz

A suggested division of responsibilities

Student A: steps 1, 2, 3, 18, 19
Student B: steps 4, 7, 8, 16, 17
Student C: steps 5, 9, 10, 12, 14
Student D: steps 6, 11, 13, 15
All students take part in step 20.

NOTES

1. Students can measure vegetable oil, tomato sauce, oregano, thyme, hot sauce, and sour cream from original containers.
2. If preferred, use boxed tortillas and eliminate steps 2 and 3.

Before class

1. Provide 4 tortillas for each group.
2. Provide a garlic clove for each group.
3. Provide a jalapeño pepper for each group.
4. Divide ground turkey into $\frac{1}{2}$-lb packages and give one to each group.
5. Divide cheese into 1-oz wedges and give a wedge to each group.

Tostadas

Makes 4 Servings

Directions

Ingredients	

4 6″ flour tortillas

1 clove garlic

1 small onion

1 jalapeño pepper

1 tbsp vegetable oil

$\frac{1}{2}$ **lb ground turkey**

$\frac{3}{4}$ **cup tomato sauce**

$\frac{3}{4}$ **tsp dried oregano**

$\frac{1}{4}$ **tsp dried thyme**

dash hot sauce

1 oz part-skim mozzarella cheese

$\frac{1}{4}$ **cup reduced-calorie sour cream**

Utensils

baking sheet

non-stick skillet

garlic press

cutting board

paring knife

wooden spoon

measuring cup

measuring spoons

cheese grater

_____ 1. Preheat oven to 350°.

_____ 2. Place **tortillas** on a baking sheet.

_____ 3. Bake 7-10 minutes until crisp.

_____ 4. Peel **garlic**. Crush and put in skillet.

_____ 5. Peel **onion**. Chop onion and add to skillet.

_____ 6. Remove seeds from **jalapeño pepper**. Chop pepper and add to skillet.

_____ 7. Add **1 tbsp vegetable oil** to the skillet.

_____ 8. Cook vegetables over medium heat until softened, stirring constantly.

_____ 9. Crumble $\frac{1}{2}$ **lb ground turkey** and add to skillet.

_____ 10. Cook over medium heat 4-5 minutes until meat is no longer pink.

_____ 11. Measure $\frac{3}{4}$ **cup tomato sauce** into skillet.

_____ 12. Measure $\frac{3}{4}$ **tsp oregano** into skillet.

_____ 13. Measure $\frac{1}{4}$ **tsp thyme** into skillet.

_____ 14. Add a **dash of hot sauce** to the skillet. Mix.

_____ 15. Spoon mixture over tortillas.

_____ 16. Grate **cheese**.

_____ 17. Sprinkle cheese over turkey mixture on each tostada.

_____ 18. Increase oven temperature to broil.

_____ 19. Broil tostadas until cheese melts.

_____ 20. Garnish each tostada with 1 tbsp of **sour cream**.

Turkey-Vegetable Roll-Ups

SHOPPING LIST

(4 students per group)	16 students	20 students	24 students	28 students	32 students
cucumbers	2	$2\frac{1}{2}$	3	$3\frac{1}{2}$	4
tomatoes	2	$2\frac{1}{2}$	3	$3\frac{1}{2}$	4
mushrooms	16	20	24	28	32
scallions	4	5	6	7	8
reduced-calorie Italian dressing	8 oz	10 oz	12 oz	14 oz	16 oz
turkey slices	32	40	48	56	64
lettuce leaves	16	20	24	28	32
mozzarella cheese	1 lb	$1\frac{1}{4}$ lb	$1\frac{1}{2}$ lb	$1\frac{3}{4}$ lb	2 lb
toothpicks	16	20	24	28	32

A suggested division of responsibilities

Student A: steps 1, 5
Student B: step 2
Student C: steps 3, 4
Student D: step 6
All students take part in steps 7, 8, 9, 10

Before class

1. Cut cucumbers in half.
2. Cut tomatoes in half.
3. Provide 4 mushrooms for each group.
4. Provide 1 scallion for each group.
5. Provide 8 slices of turkey for each group.
6. Provide 4 large lettuce leaves for each group.
7. Divide cheese into 4-oz blocks.

NOTES

1. Students can measure Italian salad dressing directly from the original container.
2. Ham can be substituted for turkey.

Turkey-Vegetable Roll-Ups

Makes 4 Servings

Directions

Ingredients

$\frac{1}{2}$ **small cucumber**

$\frac{1}{2}$ **medium tomato**

4 medium-sized mushrooms

1 scallion

$\frac{1}{4}$ **cup reduced-calorie Italian salad dressing**

8 slices prepared turkey

4 large lettuce leaves

4 oz mozzarella cheese

_____ 1. Peel skin from $\frac{1}{2}$ **small cucumber.** Chop coarsely.

_____ 2. Wash $\frac{1}{2}$ **medium tomato.** Chop coarsely.

_____ 3. Wash **4 mushrooms.** Chop coarsely.

_____ 4. Wash **1 scallion.** Slice into small pieces.

_____ 5. Combine in bowl: cucumber, tomato, mushrooms, scallion, and $\frac{1}{4}$ **cup salad dressing.** Mix well.

_____ 6. Grate **4 oz mozzarella cheese.**

_____ 7. Center **2 slices turkey** on each **lettuce leaf.**

_____ 8. Use the slotted spoon to remove vegetables from the dressing. Put one-fourth of the vegetables on each roll-up.

_____ 9. Sprinkle one-fourth of cheese on each roll-up.

_____ 10. Roll up lettuce and turkey around vegetables and cheese. Turn edges of lettuce in toward center while rolling. Fasten each roll-up with a wooden toothpick.

Utensils

small bowl

vegetable peeler

cutting board

paring knife

measuring cup

slotted spoon

cheese grater

4 toothpicks

Turkey Melts

SHOPPING LIST

(4 students per group)	16 students	20 students	24 students	28 students	32 students
whole-wheat bread	16 slices	20 slices	24 slices	28 slices	32 slices
turkey slices	16	20	24	28	32
large tomatoes	4	5	6	7	8
green pepper	2	$2\frac{1}{2}$	3	$3\frac{1}{2}$	4
cheese	8 oz	10 oz	12 oz	14 oz	16 oz

A suggested division of responsibilities

Student A: steps 1, 4

Student B: steps 2, 3, 7

Student C: steps 5, 6

Student D: steps 8, 9

Before class

1. Provide 4 slices bread for each group.

2. Provide 4 slices turkey for each group.

3. Provide 1 large tomato for each group.

4. Cut green peppers in half and give each group a piece.

5. Cut cheese into 2-oz wedges and give a wedge to each group.

Turkey Melts

Makes 4 Servings

Directions

<table>
<tr><td></td><td>Ingredients</td></tr>
<tr><td colspan="2">4 slices whole-wheat bread</td></tr>
</table>

Ingredients

4 slices whole-wheat bread

4 slices turkey

1 large tomato

$\frac{1}{2}$ **green pepper**

2 oz cheese

Utensils

toaster

baking sheet

cutting board

sharp knife

cheese grater

_____ 1. Preheat oven to broil.

_____ 2. Toast **4 slices whole-wheat bread.**

_____ 3. Arrange toast on baking sheet.

_____ 4. Place 1 slice **turkey** on each piece of toast.

_____ 5. Remove stem from **tomato**. Cut tomato into 8 slices.

_____ 6. Arrange 2 slices tomato on each sandwich.

_____ 7. Remove seeds from **green pepper**. Chop pepper finely. Divide green pepper among the 4 sandwiches.

_____ 8. Grate the **cheese**. Sprinkle over each sandwich.

_____ 9. Broil 3-5 minutes until cheese melts.

Turkey Sloppy Joes

SHOPPING LIST

(4 students per group)	16 students	20 students	24 students	28 students	32 students
small onions	4	5	6	7	8
green pepper	2	$2\frac{1}{2}$	3	$3\frac{1}{2}$	4
vegetable oil	2 oz	$2\frac{1}{2}$ oz	3 oz	$3\frac{1}{2}$ oz	4 oz
ground turkey	4 lb	5 lb	6 lb	7 lb	8 lb
8-oz cans tomato sauce	4 cans	5 cans	6 cans	7 cans	8 cans
dried basil	4 tsp	5 tsp	6 tsp	7 tsp	8 tsp
garlic powder	4 tsp	5 tsp	6 tsp	7 tsp	8 tsp
dried oregano	4 tsp	5 tsp	6 tsp	7 tsp	8 tsp
black pepper	$\frac{1}{2}$ tsp	$\frac{5}{8}$ tsp	$\frac{3}{4}$ tsp	$\frac{7}{8}$ tsp	1 tsp
hamburger buns	16	20	24	28	32

A suggested division of responsibilities

Student A: steps 1, 6, 10

Student B: steps 2, 7, 11

Student C: steps 3, 4, 8

Student D: steps 5, 9

All students take part in step 12

Before class

1. Provide an onion for each group.

2. Cut green peppers in half and give a piece to each group.

3. Provide each group with a pound of ground turkey.

4. Provide each group with an 8-oz can of tomato sauce.

5. Provide each group with 4 hamburger buns.

NOTE

1. Students can measure vegetable oil, basil, garlic powder, oregano, and black pepper from original containers.

Turkey Sloppy Joes

Makes 4 Servings

Directions

Ingredients
1 small onion
$\frac{1}{2}$ **green pepper**
1 tbsp vegetable oil
1 lb ground turkey
1 8-oz can tomato sauce
1 tsp dried basil
1 tsp garlic powder
1 tsp dried oregano
$\frac{1}{8}$ **tsp black pepper**
4 hamburger buns

_____ 1. Peel **onion**. Chop. Put in skillet.

_____ 2. Remove seeds from **green pepper**. Chop and put in skillet.

_____ 3. Add **1 tbsp vegetable oil** to skillet.

_____ 4. Cook over medium heat until vegetables are softened and water is evaporated. Stir constantly.

_____ 5. Crumble **turkey** and add to skillet. Stir mixture until turkey is heated through.

_____ 6. Add **tomato sauce** to the skillet.

_____ 7. Measure **1 tsp basil** into the skillet.

_____ 8. Measure **1 tsp garlic powder** into the skillet.

_____ 9. Measure **1 tsp oregano** into the skillet.

_____ 10. Measure $\frac{1}{8}$ **tsp black pepper** into the skillet.

_____ 11. Mix thoroughly. Cover and cook over low heat 10 minutes, stirring occasionally.

_____ 12. Spoon mixture over opened **hamburger buns**.

Utensils

cutting board
paring knife
skillet with cover
wooden spoon
can opener
measuring spoons

Meats

Barbecued Chicken

SHOPPING LIST

(4 students per group)	16 students	20 students	24 students	28 students	32 students
garlic	4 cloves	5 cloves	6 cloves	7 cloves	8 cloves
salt	1 tsp	$1\frac{1}{4}$ tsp	$1\frac{1}{2}$ tsp	$1\frac{3}{4}$ tsp	2 tsp
vinegar	4 oz	5 oz	6 oz	7 oz	8 oz
soy sauce	4 oz	5 oz	6 oz	7 oz	8 oz
Worcestershire sauce	2 oz	$2\frac{1}{2}$ oz	3 oz	$3\frac{1}{2}$ oz	4 oz
catsup	8 tsp	10 tsp	12 tsp	14 tsp	16 tsp
lemons	2	$2\frac{1}{2}$	3	$3\frac{1}{2}$	4
tomato juice	24 oz	30 oz	36 oz	42 oz	48 oz
chicken thighs	16	20	24	28	32
chicken drumsticks	16	20	24	28	32

A suggested division of responsibilities

Student A: steps 2, 6, 7, 9

Student B: steps 3, 4, 5, 8, 10, 11

Student C: steps 1, 13, 16, 17

Student D: steps 12, 14, 15

Before class

1. Provide each group with a garlic clove.

2. Cut lemons in half and give half a lemon to each group.

3. Provide each group with 4 chicken thighs and 4 drumsticks.

NOTES

1. Students can measure salt, vinegar, soy sauce, Worcestershire sauce, catsup, and tomato juice from original containers.

2. This sauce can be made ahead and stored in the refrigerator for several days.

3. If time is a problem, eliminate step 14. Have students begin to cook chicken (step 15) without sauce. Then add the sauce (step 16) and finish cooking (step 17).

Barbecued Chicken

Makes 4 Servings

Directions

Ingredients

1 clove garlic

$\frac{1}{4}$ **tsp salt**

2 tbsp vinegar

2 tbsp soy sauce

1 tbsp Worcestershire sauce

2 tsp catsup

$\frac{1}{2}$ **lemon**

$\frac{3}{4}$ **cup tomato juice**

4 chicken thighs

4 chicken drumsticks

Utensils

garlic press

measuring spoons

small saucepan

wooden spoon

can opener

measuring cup

broiler pan

aluminum foil

fork

_____ 1. Preheat oven to broil.

_____ 2. Peel **garlic clove** and crush. Put in saucepan.

_____ 3. Measure $\frac{1}{4}$ **tsp salt** into saucepan.

_____ 4. Measure **2 tbsp vinegar** into saucepan.

_____ 5. Measure **2 tbsp soy sauce** into saucepan.

_____ 6. Measure **1 tbsp Worcestershire sauce** into saucepan.

_____ 7. Measure **2 tsp catsup** into saucepan.

_____ 8. Squeeze $\frac{1}{2}$ **lemon**. Add juice to saucepan.

_____ 9. Mix ingredients well.

_____ 10. Add $\frac{3}{4}$ **cup tomato juice** to the saucepan. Mix.

_____ 11. Cook over moderate heat, stirring frequently. When sauce begins to thicken (10-15 minutes), remove from heat.

_____ 12. Line broiler pan with aluminum foil.

_____ 13. Arrange **chicken** on the pan.

_____ 14. Pour half the sauce over the chicken.

_____ 15. Broil 7 inches from the heat source for 10 minutes.

_____ 16. Turn chicken. Pour remainder of sauce over chicken.

_____ 17. Broil 10 minutes longer.

Oriental Pork Chops

SHOPPING LIST

(4 students per group)	16 students	20 students	24 students	28 students	32 students
pork chops (thin)	16	20	24	28	32
4-oz cans mushrooms	4 cans	5 cans	6 cans	7 cans	8 cans
celery	8 stalks	10 stalks	12 stalks	14 stalks	16 stalks
small onions	4	5	6	7	8
soy sauce	2 oz	$2\frac{1}{2}$ oz	3 oz	$3\frac{1}{2}$ oz	4 oz
chicken bouillon	4 tsp	5 tsp	6 tsp	7 tsp	8 tsp
cornstarch	8 tsp	10 tsp	12 tsp	14 tsp	16 tsp
water chestnuts (canned)	32	40	48	56	64

A suggested division of responsibilities

Student A: steps 1, 2, 3, 4, 15

Student B: steps 5, 6, 7, 17, 18

Student C: steps 8, 9, 10, 11, 19

Student D: steps 12, 13, 14, 16

Before class

1. Provide each group with 4 pork chops.

2. Provide each group with a 4-oz can of sliced mushrooms.

3. Provide each group with 2 stalks of celery.

4. Provide each group with a small onion.

5. Provide each group with 8 water chestnuts.

NOTE

1. Students can measure water, soy sauce, bouillon, and cornstarch from original containers.

Oriental Pork Chops

Makes 4 Servings

Ingredients

4 thin pork chops

$\frac{1}{2}$ **cup water**

1 4-oz can sliced mushrooms

2 stalks celery

1 small onion

1 tbsp soy sauce

1 tsp chicken bouillon

2 tsp cornstarch

$\frac{1}{4}$ **cup cold water**

8 water chestnuts (canned)

Utensils

non-stick skillet with cover
fork
measuring cup
can opener
cutting board
paring knife
measuring spoons
wooden spoon
small bowl
mixing spoon

Directions

_____ 1. Heat skillet over medium heat.

_____ 2. Put **pork chops** in skillet and brown.

_____ 3. Turn pork chops to brown other side.

_____ 4. Drain any grease from the skillet.

_____ 5. Measure $\frac{1}{2}$ **cup water** into the skillet.

_____ 6. Drain the **mushrooms** and add to the skillet.

_____ 7. Trim **celery stalks**. Slice celery and add to skillet.

_____ 8. Peel **onion**. Slice onion and add to skillet.

_____ 9. Measure **1 tbsp soy sauce** into skillet.

_____ 10. Measure **1 tsp chicken bouillon** into skillet.

_____ 11. Cover skillet and simmer 10-15 minutes until vegetables are tender.

_____ 12. Measure **2 tsp cornstarch** into small bowl.

_____ 13. Add $\frac{1}{4}$ **cup cold water** to cornstarch.

_____ 15. Remove pork chops from skillet.

_____ 16. Add cornstarch mixture to skillet. Stir.

_____ 17. Slice **water chestnuts** and add to skillet.

_____ 18. Stir until mixture is thick and bubbly.

_____ 19. Pour sauce over pork chops.

Light and Tasty Cooking Labs

Tuna Loaf

SHOPPING LIST

(4 students per group)	16 students	20 students	24 students	28 students	32 students
celery	8 stalks	10 stalks	12 stalks	14 stalks	16 stalks
green onions	8	10	12	14	16
$6\frac{1}{2}$-oz cans tuna, water-packed	4 cans	5 cans	6 cans	7 cans	8 cans
whole-wheat bread	4 slices	5 slices	6 slices	7 slices	8 slices
eggs	4	5	6	7	8
plain low-fat yogurt	4 oz	5 oz	6 oz	7 oz	8 oz
horseradish	4 tsp	5 tsp	6 tsp	7 tsp	8 tsp
dry mustard	2 tsp	$2\frac{1}{2}$ tsp	3 tsp	$3\frac{1}{2}$ tsp	4 tsp
margarine	2 tsp	$2\frac{1}{2}$ tsp	3 tsp	$3\frac{1}{2}$ tsp	4 tsp

A suggested division of responsibilities

Student A: steps 1, 4, 5, 13

Student B: steps 2, 8, 10, 14

Student C: steps 3, 9, 11, 15

Student D: steps 6, 7, 12

Before class

1. Provide each group with 2 stalks of celery.

2. Provide each group with 2 green onions.

3. Provide each group with a can of tuna.

4. Provide each group with a slice of bread.

5. Provide each group with an egg.

NOTES

1. Students can measure yogurt, horseradish, mustard, and margarine from original containers.

2. Instead of making individual servings, the tuna mixture can be baked in a small bowl or casserole dish.

Tuna Loaf

Makes 4 Servings

Directions

Ingredients
2 stalks celery
2 green onions
1 6½-oz can tuna, packed in water
1 slice whole-wheat bread
1 egg
2 tbsp plain low-fat yogurt
1 tsp horseradish
½ tsp dry mustard
½ tsp margarine

_____ 1. Preheat oven to 350°.

_____ 2. Trim **celery**. Chop fine and put in skillet.

_____ 3. Trim **green onions**. Chop fine and add to skillet.

_____ 4. Add 2-3 tbsp water to skillet.

_____ 5. Cook over medium heat, stirring constantly, until vegetables are softened. Remove from heat.

_____ 6. Drain **tuna**. Add to skillet.

_____ 7. Break **bread** into fine bread crumbs. Add to skillet.

_____ 8. Break **egg** into the skillet.

_____ 9. Measure **2 tbsp yogurt** into the skillet.

_____ 10. Measure **1 tsp horseradish** into skillet.

_____ 11. Measure **½ tsp dry mustard** into skillet.

_____ 12. Mix all ingredients well.

_____ 13. Use the **margarine** to lightly grease 4 custard cups.

_____ 14. Divide tuna mixture among the 4 custard cups.

_____ 15. Bake for 15 minutes. Serve hot.

Utensils

cutting board

paring knife

skillet

wooden spoon

can opener

measuring spoons

mixing spoon

4 custard cups

Turkey Sausage

SHOPPING LIST

(4 students per group)	16 students	20 students	24 students	28 students	32 students
ground turkey	4 lb	5 lb	6 lb	7 lb	8 lb
salt	2 tsp	$2\frac{1}{2}$ tsp	3 tsp	$3\frac{1}{2}$ tsp	4 tsp
black pepper	2 tsp	$2\frac{1}{2}$ tsp	3 tsp	$3\frac{1}{2}$ tsp	4 tsp
sage	4 tsp	5 tsp	6 tsp	7 tsp	8 tsp
fennel	2 tsp	$2\frac{1}{2}$ tsp	3 tsp	$3\frac{1}{2}$ tsp	4 tsp

A suggested division of responsibilities

Student A: steps 1, 9

Student B: steps 2, 5

Student C: steps 3, 6

Student D: steps 4, 7

All students take part in step 8

Before class

1. Provide each group with 1 lb of ground turkey.

NOTES

1. Students can measure salt, black pepper, sage, and fennel from the original containers.

2. Flavor will be best if sausage can be refrigerated a few hours or overnight to let the flavor develop, but it can be cooked immediately.

3. A variety of different herbs and spices can be used to make sausage from ground turkey.

Turkey Sausage

Makes 4 Servings

Directions

Ingredients

1 lb ground turkey

$\frac{1}{2}$ tsp salt

$\frac{1}{2}$ tsp black pepper

1 tsp sage

$\frac{1}{2}$ tsp fennel

_____ 1. Crumble **ground turkey** and put it in the bowl.

_____ 2. Measure $\frac{1}{2}$ **tsp salt** into the bowl.

_____ 3. Measure $\frac{1}{2}$ **tsp black pepper** into the bowl.

_____ 4. Measure **1 tsp sage** into the bowl.

_____ 5. Measure $\frac{1}{2}$ **tsp fennel** into the bowl.

_____ 6. Mix ingredients together very thoroughly.

_____ 7. Divide into 8 equal amounts.

_____ 8. Shape each part into a sausage patty.

_____ 9. Cook in frying pan over medium heat. Turn once. Do not overcook.

Utensils

bowl

measuring spoons

mixing spoon

frying pan

spatula

paper towels

Vegetables and Salads

Baked Potato Chips

SHOPPING LIST

(4 students per group)	16 students	20 students	24 students	28 students	32 students
margarine	8 tsp	10 tsp	4 tbsp	14 tsp	16 tsp
potatoes	16	20	24	28	32
powdered garlic	16 tsp	20 tsp	8 tbsp	28 tsp	32 tsp
paprika	16 tsp	20 tsp	8 tbsp	28 tsp	32 tsp

A suggested division of responsibilities

    Student A: step 1

    Student B: step 2

    Student C: step 3

    Student D: step 9

    All students take part in steps 4, 5, 6, 7, 8

Before class

1. Provide each student with a potato.

NOTES

1. Students can measure margarine, powdered garlic, and paprika from the original containers.

2. If cut potatoes are left in the air, they will discolor. To avoid this, put cut potatoes in cold water.

3. If a large number of potato chips are being prepared, using a food processor to cut the potatoes would be fast and would assure even thickness.

4. Other herbs or seasonings can be used. If students really miss the salt, try using reduced-sodium salt on the potato chips.

Baked Potato Chips

Makes 4 Servings

Directions

Ingredients

$\frac{1}{2}$ tsp margarine

1 large potato

1 tsp powdered garlic (approx.)

1 tsp paprika (approx.)

_____ 1. Preheat oven to 400°.

_____ 2. Line the baking sheet with aluminum foil.

_____ 3. Using the paper towel, lightly rub the $\frac{1}{2}$ tsp margarine over the foil to keep the potatoes from sticking.

_____ 4. Wash the **potato**.

_____ 5. Leaving the skin on, cut the potato into thin slices.

_____ 6. Spread the potato slices on the baking sheet.

_____ 7. Sprinkle the potatoes with **powdered garlic**.

_____ 8. Sprinkle the potatoes with **paprika**.

_____ 9. Bake 10 to 20 minutes. The thinnest potatoes may be done in 10 minutes. Thicker potatoes may take as long as 20 minutes. Remove potatoes from the pan as they turn brown and crispy.

Utensils

baking sheet
aluminum foil
paper towel
paring knife

Cinnamon-Apple Squash

SHOPPING LIST

(4 students per group)	16 students	20 students	24 students	28 students	32 students
winter squash	4	5	6	7	8
apples	8	10	12	14	16
cinnamon	4 tsp	5 tsp	6 tsp	7 tsp	8 tsp

A suggested division of responsibilities

    Student A: steps 1, 5, 9

    Student B: steps 2, 6, 10

    Student C: steps 3, 7

    Student D: steps 4, 8

Before class

1. Provide each group with a small squash.

2. Provide each group with 2 apples.

NOTES

1. Students can measure cinnamon from the original container.

2. If a Hubbard or other large squash is what is available, it will work fine. Jut cut it into appropriate-sized pieces for each group to use.

Cinnamon-Apple Squash

Makes 4 Servings

Directions

Ingredients

1 small winter squash (buttercup, acorn, butternut, etc.)

2 cooking apples

1 tsp cinnamon

Utensils

paring knife
cutting board
saucepan with cover
measuring spoons
electric mixer

_____ 1. Cut **squash** into quarters. Remove seeds and peel squash.

_____ 2. Cut squash into 1″ pieces and put in saucepan.

_____ 3. Cut **apples** in quarters. Remove core and peel.

_____ 4. Slice apples and add to saucepan.

_____ 5. Add water to just cover squash and apples.

_____ 6. Cover and cook over medium heat 15-20 minutes until squash and apples are tender.

_____ 7. Drain water from saucepan.

_____ 8. Measure **1 tsp cinnamon** into saucepan with squash and apples.

_____ 9. Use electric mixer to mash and blend ingredients.

_____ 10. Serve hot.

Cucumber-Orange Salad

SHOPPING LIST

(4 students per group)	16 students	20 students	24 students	28 students	32 students
cucumbers	4	5	6	7	8
oranges	8	10	12	14	16
green peppers	2	$2\frac{1}{2}$	3	$3\frac{1}{2}$	4
fresh mint	8 stems	10 stems	12 stems	14 stems	16 stems
plain low-fat yogurt	$1\frac{1}{3}$ cups	$1\frac{2}{3}$ cups	2 cups	$2\frac{1}{3}$ cups	$2\frac{2}{3}$ cups
dried thyme	1 tsp	$1\frac{1}{4}$ tsp	$1\frac{1}{2}$ tsp	$1\frac{3}{4}$ tsp	2 tsp
lettuce leaves	16	20	24	28	32

A suggested division of responsibilities

    Student A: steps 1, 4

    Student B: steps 2, 8

    Student C: steps 3, 9

    Student D: steps 5, 6, 7

    All students will take part in step 10

Before class

1. Provide each group with a cucumber.

2. Provide each group with 2 oranges.

3. Cut green peppers in half and give a piece to each group.

4. Provide each group with 2 stems of fresh mint.

5. Provide each group with 4 lettuce leaves.

NOTE

1. Students can measure yogurt and thyme from original containers.

Cucumber-Orange Salad

Makes 4 Servings

Directions

Ingredients

1 medium cucumber

2 medium oranges

$\frac{1}{2}$ **green pepper**

2 stems fresh mint

$\frac{1}{3}$ **cup plain low-fat yogurt**

$\frac{1}{4}$ **tsp dried thyme**

4 lettuce leaves

_____ 1. Trim ends from **cucumber**. Cut cucumber into very thin slices. Put in bowl.

_____ 2. Peel **oranges** and divide into sections. Add to bowl.

_____ 3. Remove seeds from **green pepper**. Chop green pepper and add to bowl.

_____ 4. Chop fresh mint. Add **2 tbsp mint** to the bowl.

_____ 5. Measure $\frac{1}{3}$ **cup yogurt** into the small bowl.

_____ 6. Measure $\frac{1}{4}$ **tsp thyme** into the small bowl.

_____ 7. Mix dressing.

_____ 8. Add dressing to large bowl. Stir gently.

_____ 9. Wash **lettuce leaves**.

_____ 10. Spoon one-fourth of the salad onto each lettuce leaf.

Utensils

medium bowl

cutting board

paring knife

measuring cup

measuring spoons

small bowl

mixing spoon

Dilly Bean Salad

SHOPPING LIST

(4 students per group)	16 students	20 students	24 students	28 students	32 students
fresh green beans	4 lb	5 lb	6 lb	7 lb	8 lb
red wine vinegar	4 oz	5 oz	6 oz	7 oz	8 oz
lemon juice	2 oz	$2\frac{1}{2}$ oz	3 oz	$3\frac{1}{2}$ oz	4 oz
dried dillweed	8 tsp	10 tsp	12 tsp	14 tsp	16 tsp
dried parsley	2 tsp	$2\frac{1}{2}$ tsp	3 tsp	$3\frac{1}{2}$ tsp	4 tsp
Dijon mustard	4 tsp	5 tsp	6 tsp	7 tsp	8 tsp
sugar	4 tsp	5 tsp	2 tbsp	7 tsp	8 tsp

A suggested division of responsibilities

Student A: steps 1 (with B), 2, 3
Student B: steps 1 (with A), 4, 5
Student C: steps 6, 8, 10, 12
Student D: steps 7, 9, 11, 13

Before Class

1. Provide each group with 1 lb of green beans.

NOTES

1. Students can measure vinegar, lemon juice, dillweed, parsley, mustard, and sugar from the original containers.

2. This dish can also be served hot. Don't rinse the beans in cold water. Return to the saucepan. Add the dressing and heat through.

Dilly Bean Salad

Makes 4 Servings

Directions

Ingredients

1 lb fresh green beans

2 tbsp red wine vinegar

1 tbsp lemon juice

2 tsp dried dillweed

$\frac{1}{2}$ tsp dried parsley

1 tsp Dijon mustard

1 tsp sugar

_____ 1. Trim ends of **beans**. Cut beans into pieces $1\frac{1}{2}''$ long.

_____ 2. Place beans in saucepan. Cover with water.

_____ 3. Cook over medium heat 5-10 minutes until tender but still crisp.

_____ 4. Drain beans in colander. Rinse with cold water.

_____ 5. Put beans in medium bowl.

_____ 6. Measure **2 tbsp red wine vinegar** into small bowl.

_____ 7. Measure **1 tbsp lemon juice** into small bowl.

_____ 8. Measure **2 tsp dillweed** into small bowl.

_____ 9. Measure **$\frac{1}{2}$ tsp parsley** into small bowl.

_____ 10. Measure **1 tsp mustard** into small bowl.

_____ 11. Measure **1 tsp sugar** into small bowl.

_____ 12. Use a wire whisk to combine the dressing ingredients.

_____ 13. Pour the dressing over the beans. Mix well.

Utensils

saucepan

colander

medium bowl

small bowl

wire whisk

measuring spoons

mixing spoon

Light and Tasty Cooking Labs

Greek Potato Salad

SHOPPING LIST

(4 students per group)	16 students	20 students	24 students	28 students	32 students
potatoes	12	15	18	21	24
cucumbers	2	$2\frac{1}{2}$	3	$3\frac{1}{2}$	4
cherry tomatoes	16	20	24	28	32
reduced-calorie mayonnaise	1 cup	$1\frac{1}{4}$ cups	$1\frac{1}{2}$ cups	$1\frac{3}{4}$ cups	2 cups
garlic	4 cloves	5 cloves	6 cloves	7 cloves	8 cloves
feta cheese	8 tbsp	10 tbsp	12 tbsp	14 tbsp	16 tbsp
dried parsley	4 tsp	5 tsp	6 tsp	7 tsp	8 tsp
dried oregano	1 tsp	$1\frac{1}{4}$ tsp	$1\frac{1}{2}$ tsp	$1\frac{3}{4}$ tsp	2 tsp
dried rosemary	$\frac{1}{2}$ tsp	$\frac{5}{8}$ tsp	$\frac{3}{4}$ tsp	$\frac{7}{8}$ tsp	1 tsp
black pepper	4 dashes	5 dashes	6 dashes	7 dashes	8 dashes
ripe olives (optional)	16	20	24	28	32

A suggested division of responsibilities

Student A: steps 1, 12, 13
Student B: steps 2, 3
Student C: steps 4, 6, 8, 10
Student D: steps 5, 7, 9, 11

NOTES

1. Students can measure mayonnaise, parsley, oregano, rosemary, and black pepper from original containers.

2. If preferred, students can peel potatoes before putting them in the salad.

Before class

Cook 1. Cook potatoes. Provide 3 potatoes for each group.

2. Cut cucumbers in half. Give half a cucumber to each group.

3. Provide 4 cherry tomatoes for each group.

4. Provide a garlic clove for each group.

5. Divide feta cheese into 2-tbsp packages and give a package to each group.

6. If desired, provide each group with 4 ripe olives.

Greek Potato Salad

Makes 4 Servings

Directions

Ingredients

3 medium-sized potatoes (cooked in skins)

$\frac{1}{2}$ **small cucumber**

4 cherry tomatoes

$\frac{1}{4}$ **cup reduced-calorie mayonnaise**

1 clove garlic

2 tbsp feta cheese

1 tsp dried parsley

$\frac{1}{4}$ **tsp dried oregano**

$\frac{1}{8}$ **tsp dried rosemary**

dash black pepper

4 ripe olives (optional)

_____ 1. Cut **potatoes** into cubes. Put in bowl.

_____ 2. Peel $\frac{1}{2}$ **cucumber**. Chop and put in bowl.

_____ 3. Remove stems from **tomatoes**. Cut in quarters and add to bowl.

_____ 4. Measure $\frac{1}{4}$ **cup mayonnaise** into blender.

_____ 5. Peel **garlic clove**. Slice and put in blender.

_____ 6. Crumble **2 tbsp feta cheese** into blender.

_____ 7. Measure **1 tsp parsley** into blender.

_____ 8. Measure $\frac{1}{4}$ **tsp oregano** into blender.

_____ 9. Measure $\frac{1}{8}$ **tsp rosemary** into blender.

_____ 10. Sprinkle **black pepper** into blender.

_____ 11. Put cover on blender. Blend until smooth.

_____ 12. Add dressing to vegetables. Stir gently.

_____ 13. If desired, garnish salad with sliced **ripe olives**.

Utensils

bowl
paring knife
cutting board
blender
measuring spoons
mixing spoon

Herb-Baked Tomatoes

SHOPPING LIST

(4 students per group)	16 students	20 students	24 students	28 students	32 students
tomatoes	8	10	12	14	16
bread crumbs	8 tbsp	10 tbsp	12 tbsp	14 tbsp	16 tbsp
fresh parsley	8-12 stems	10-14 stems	12-16 stems	14-18 stems	16-20 stems
fresh thyme	4 stems	5 stems	6 stems	7 stems	8 stems
Parmesan cheese	4 tbsp	5 tbsp	6 tbsp	7 tbsp	8 tbsp

A suggested division of responsibilities

Student A: steps 1, 4
Student B: steps 2, 8
Student C: steps 3, 9
Student D: steps 5, 6, 7

Before class

1. Provide each group with 2 tomatoes.

2. Provide each group with 2 or 3 stems of fresh parsley.

3. Provide each group with 1 stem of fresh thyme.

NOTE

1. Students can measure bread crumbs and Parmesan cheese from original containers.

Herb-Baked Tomatoes

Makes 4 Servings

Directions

Ingredients

2 large tomatoes

2 tbsp bread crumbs

2 or 3 stems parsley

1 stem fresh thyme

1 tbsp Parmesan cheese

Utensils

baking sheet
sharp knife
cutting board
small bowl
measuring spoons
mixing spoon

_____ 1. Preheat oven to 400°.

_____ 2. Slice **tomatoes**. Place on baking sheet.

_____ 3. Wash parsley. Chop very finely and measure **2 tsp of parsley** into the bowl.

_____ 4. Wash thyme. Chop very finely and measure $\frac{1}{2}$ **tsp of thyme** into the bowl.

_____ 5. Measure **2 tbsp bread crumbs** into the bowl.

_____ 6. Measure **1 tbsp Parmesan cheese** into the bowl.

_____ 7. Mix the ingredients in the bowl.

_____ 8. Sprinkle the crumb mixture over the tomatoes.

_____ 9. Bake 10 to 12 minutes.

Nutty Cabbage

SHOPPING LIST

(4 students per group)	16 students	20 students	24 students	28 students	32 students
chicken bouillon	8 tsp	10 tsp	12 tsp	14 tsp	16 tsp
cabbage	2 heads	$2\frac{1}{2}$ heads	3 heads	$3\frac{1}{2}$ heads	4 heads
carrots	8	10	12	14	16
green onions	8	10	12	14	16
dill seed	2 tsp	$2\frac{1}{2}$ tsp	3 tsp	$3\frac{1}{2}$ tsp	4 tsp
pecans or other nuts	36-40	45-50	54-60	63-70	72-80
plain low-fat yogurt	4 oz	5 oz	6 oz	7 oz	8 oz
honey	4 tsp	5 tsp	6 tsp	7 tsp	8 tsp
prepared mustard	2 tsp	$2\frac{1}{2}$ tsp	3 tsp	$3\frac{1}{2}$ tsp	4 tsp

A suggested division of responsibilities

    Student A: steps 1, 2, 3, 6
    Student B: steps 4, 7, 15, 16
    Student C: steps 5, 8, 9
    Student D: steps 10, 11, 12, 13, 14

Before class

1. Cut cabbage heads in half and provide half a cabbage to each group.

2. Provide each group with 2 carrots.

3. Provide each group with 2 green onions.

4. Provide each group with 9 or 10 pecans or other nuts.

NOTE

1. Students can measure water, bouillon, dill seed, yogurt, honey, and mustard from the original containers.

Nutty Cabbage

Makes 4 Servings

Directions

Ingredients

$\frac{1}{3}$ **cup water**

2 tsp chicken bouillon

$\frac{1}{2}$ **head cabbage**

2 carrots

2 green onions

$\frac{1}{2}$ **tsp dill seed**

9 or 10 pecans or other nuts

2 tbsp plain low-fat yogurt

1 tsp honey

$\frac{1}{2}$ **tsp prepared mustard**

_____ 1. Measure $\frac{1}{3}$ **cup water** into saucepan.

_____ 2. Measure **2 tsp chicken bouillon** into saucepan.

_____ 3. Heat over medium heat until bouillon dissolves.

_____ 4. Shred **cabbage** coarsely. Add to saucepan.

_____ 5. Peel **carrots**. Grate carrots and add to saucepan.

_____ 6. Trim **green onions**. Chop onions and add to saucepan.

_____ 7. Measure $\frac{1}{2}$ **tsp dill seed** into saucepan.

_____ 8. Stir ingredients in saucepan.

_____ 9. Cover saucepan. Cook over medium heat about 5 minutes or until vegetables are tender-crisp.

_____ 10. Chop nuts finely. Measure **3 tbsp chopped nuts** into small bowl.

_____ 11. Measure **2 tbsp yogurt** into bowl.

_____ 12. Measure **1 tsp honey** into bowl.

_____ 13. Measure $\frac{1}{2}$ **tsp mustard** into bowl.

_____ 14. Mix ingredients in bowl together.

_____ 15. Drain cooked vegetables.

_____ 16. Add sauce to vegetables and mix well. Serve hot.

Utensils

saucepan with cover

grater

vegetable peeler

cutting board

paring knife

measuring spoons

wooden spoon

small bowl

mixing spoon

Light and Tasty Cooking Labs

Parmesan Steamed Vegetables

SHOPPING LIST

(4 students per group)	16 students	20 students	24 students	28 students	32 students
carrots	8	10	12	14	16
cauliflower	1 head	$1\frac{1}{4}$ heads	$1\frac{1}{2}$ heads	$1\frac{3}{4}$ heads	2 heads
broccoli	4 stems	5 stems	6 stems	7 stems	8 stems
Parmesan cheese	8 tbsp	10 tbsp	12 tbsp	14 tbsp	16 tbsp

A suggested division of responsibilities

    Student A: steps 1, 7, 8

    Student B: steps 2, 3

    Student C: steps 4, 5

    Student D: step 6

NOTE

1. Students can measure cheese from original container.

Before class

1. Provide each group with 2 carrots.

2. Cut cauliflower heads in quarters. Give a piece to each group.

3. Provide each group with a stem of broccoli.

Parmesan Steamed Vegetables

Makes 4 Servings

Directions

	Ingredients

2 carrots

$\frac{1}{4}$ **head cauliflower**

1 stem broccoli

**2 tbsp grated
    Parmesan cheese**

Utensils

saucepan with cover

vegetable steamer basket

vegetable peeler

cutting board

paring knife

measuring spoons

serving dish

_____ 1. Put 1 inch of water in bottom of saucepan and heat to a boil.

_____ 2. Peel **carrots**. Slice carrots on the bias to make oval slices. Put carrot slices in the steamer basket.

_____ 3. Place basket over boiling water. Cover and steam for 5 minutes.

_____ 4. Remove core from **cauliflower**. Cut cauliflower into flowerets.

_____ 5. Add cauliflower to basket. Cover and steam 10 minutes longer.

_____ 6. Cut **broccoli** flowerets. Add to steamer. Cover and cook 5 minutes longer until all vegetables are tender-crisp.

_____ 7. Put vegetables on a serving dish.

_____ 8. Sprinkle with **2 tbsp grated Parmesan cheese**.

Pineapple Carrots

SHOPPING LIST

(4 students per group)	16 students	20 students	24 students	28 students	32 students
crushed pineapple (juice-packed)	16 oz	20 oz	24 oz	28 oz	32 oz
carrots	16	20	24	28	32
cornstarch	4 tsp	5 tsp	6 tsp	7 tsp	8 tsp
fresh parsley	4 stems	5 stems	6 stems	7 stems	8 stems

A suggested division of responsibilities

Student A: steps 1, 2, 3, 10
Student B: steps 4 (with C), 5
Student C: steps 4 (with B), 6
Student D: steps 7, 8, 9, 11

Before class

1. Provide each group with 4 carrots.
2. Provide each group with 1 stem of parsley.

NOTES

1. Two groups can share each 8-oz can of crushed pineapple.
2. Students can measure water and cornstarch from original containers.

Pineapple Carrots

Makes 4 Servings

Directions

Ingredients

4 oz crushed pineapple (packed in its own juice)

$\frac{1}{2}$ **cup water**

4 carrots

1 tsp cornstarch

1 stem parsley

Utensils

can opener
small bowl
measuring spoons
suacepan with cover
vegetable peeler
cutting board
paring knife
mixing spoon

_____ 1. Drain **pineapple**. Reserve 2 tbsp juice in the small bowl.

_____ 2. Put pineapple in the saucepan.

_____ 3. Add $\frac{1}{2}$ **cup water** to the saucepan.

_____ 4. Peel **carrots**. Cut carrots into julienne strips. (Cut each carrot crosswise into 3 or 4 pieces and then cut each piece into thin strips.)

_____ 5. Add carrots to the saucepan.

_____ 6. Cover saucepan and cook 12 to 15 minutes over medium heat until carrots are tender.

_____ 7. Measure **1 tsp cornstarch** into small bowl with the pineapple juice. Mix.

_____ 8. Add cornstarch mixture to the cooked carrots and pineapple.

_____ 9. Cook and stir over low heat until bubbly.

_____ 10. Chop **parsley**. Add to saucepan and mix.

_____ 11. Serve warm.

Rainbow Slaw

SHOPPING LIST

(4 students per group)	16 students	20 students	24 students	28 students	32 students
cauliflower	1 head	$1\frac{1}{4}$ heads	$1\frac{1}{2}$ heads	$1\frac{3}{4}$ heads	2 heads
carrots	4	5	6	7	8
red cabbage	1 head	$1\frac{1}{4}$ heads	$1\frac{1}{2}$ heads	$1\frac{3}{4}$ heads	2 heads
green peppers	1	$1\frac{1}{4}$	$1\frac{1}{2}$	$1\frac{3}{4}$	2
green onions	8	10	12	14	16
fresh parsley	8 stems	10 stems	12 stems	14 stems	16 stems
reduced-calorie mayonnaise	6 oz	$7\frac{1}{2}$ oz	9 oz	$10\frac{1}{2}$ oz	12 oz
plain low-fat yogurt	6 oz	$7\frac{1}{2}$ oz	9 oz	$10\frac{1}{2}$ oz	12 oz
lemons	1	$1\frac{1}{4}$	$1\frac{1}{2}$	$1\frac{3}{4}$	2
dried basil	2 tsp	$2\frac{1}{2}$ tsp	3 tsp	$3\frac{1}{2}$ tsp	4 tsp
dried dillweed	2 tsp	$2\frac{1}{2}$ tsp	3 tsp	$3\frac{1}{2}$ tsp	4 tsp
dried tarragon	2 tsp	$2\frac{1}{2}$ tsp	3 tsp	$3\frac{1}{2}$ tsp	4 tsp
honey	4 tsp	5 tsp	2 tbsp	7 tsp	8 tsp

A suggested division of responsibilities

Student A: steps 1, 5, 15
Student B: steps 2, 6
Student C: steps 3, 7, 9, 11, 13
Student D: steps 4, 8, 10, 12, 14

NOTE

1. Students can measure mayonnaise, yogurt, basil, dillweed, and tarragon from the original containers.

Before class

1. Cuts heads of cauliflower in quarters and give one piece to each group.
2. Provide each group with a carrot.
3. Cut heads of cabbage in quarters and provide each group with a piece.
4. Cut green peppers in quarters and provide each group with a piece.
5. Provide each group with 2 green onions.
6. Provide each group with 2 stems of fresh parsley.
7. Cut lemons in quarters and provide each group with a piece.

Rainbow Slaw

Makes 4 Servings

Directions

Ingredients

$\frac{1}{4}$ **small head cauliflower**

1 carrot

$\frac{1}{4}$ **small head red cabbage**

$\frac{1}{4}$ **large green pepper**

2 green onions

2 stems fresh parsley

3 tbsp reduced-calorie mayonnaise

3 tbsp plain low-fat yogurt

$\frac{1}{4}$ **lemon**

$\frac{1}{2}$ **tsp dried basil**

$\frac{1}{2}$ **tsp dried dillweed**

$\frac{1}{2}$ **tsp dried tarragon**

1 tsp honey

_____ 1. Remove core from **cauliflower**. Chop cauliflower and put in large bowl.

_____ 2. Peel **carrot**. Shred carrot and add to bowl.

_____ 3. Remove core from **cabbage**. Chop cabbage and add to bowl.

_____ 4. Remove seeds from **green pepper**. Chop and add to bowl.

_____ 5. Trim **green onions**. Chop and add to bowl.

_____ 6. Chop **fresh parsley**. Add to bowl.

_____ 7. Measure **3 tbsp reduced-calorie mayonnaise** into small bowl.

_____ 8. Measure **3 tbsp yogurt** into small bowl.

_____ 9. Squeeze juice of $\frac{1}{4}$ **lemon** into small bowl.

_____ 10. Measure $\frac{1}{2}$ **tsp basil** into small bowl.

_____ 11. Measure $\frac{1}{2}$ **tsp dillweed** into small bowl.

_____ 12. Measure $\frac{1}{2}$ **tsp tarragon** into small bowl.

_____ 13. Measure **1 tsp honey** into small bowl.

_____ 14. Mix ingredients in small bowl thoroughly.

_____ 15. Pour dressing on vegetables. Toss well.

Utensils

cutting board
sharp knife
vegetable peeler
grater
large bowl
measuring spoons
small bowl
mixing spoon

129

Light and Tasty Cooking Labs

Sesame Broccoli

SHOPPING LIST

(4 students per group)	16 students	20 students	24 students	28 students	32 students
broccoli	4 lb	5 lb	6 lb	7 lb	8 lb
sesame seeds	4 tbsp	5 tbsp	6 tbsp	7 tbsp	8 tbsp
vinegar	2 oz	$2\frac{1}{2}$ oz	3 oz	$3\frac{1}{2}$ oz	4 oz
soy sauce	2 oz	$2\frac{1}{2}$ oz	3 oz	$3\frac{1}{2}$ oz	4 oz
honey	2 oz	$2\frac{1}{2}$ oz	3 oz	$3\frac{1}{2}$ oz	4 oz

A suggested division of responsibilities

Student A: steps 1, 6, 7, 13

Student B: steps 2, 4, 14

Student C: steps 3, 5, 15

Student D: steps 8, 9, 10, 11, 12

Before class

1. Provide each group with 1 lb of fresh broccoli.

NOTE

1. Students can measure sesame seeds, vinegar, soy sauce, honey, and water from the original containers.

Sesame Broccoli

Makes 4 Servings

Ingredients

1 lb fresh broccoli

1 tbsp sesame seeds

1 tbsp vinegar

1 tbsp soy sauce

1 tbsp honey

1 tbsp water

Utensils

large saucepan with cover
cutting board
paring knife
measuring spoons
baking pan
small saucepan
wooden spoon

Directions

_____ 1. Preheat oven to 375°.

_____ 2. Put 1 inch of water in the large saucepan. Heat water to a boil.

_____ 3. Wash **broccoli**. Cut off outer leaves and tough part of stems.

_____ 4. Cut broccoli lengthwise to make long spears.

_____ 5. Add broccoli to boiling water. Cover and cook 10-12 minutes until broccoli is crisp-tender.

_____ 6. Measure **1 tbsp sesame seeds** into baking pan.

_____ 7. Toast sesame seeds in the oven 4-5 minutes. Check frequently to be sure they do not burn.

_____ 8. Measure **1 tbsp vinegar** into the small saucepan.

_____ 9. Measure **1 tbsp soy sauce** into the small saucepan.

_____ 10. Measure **1 tbsp honey** into the small saucepan.

_____ 11. Measure **1 tbsp water** into the small saucepan.

_____ 12. Stir and heat to a boil.

_____ 13. Add sesame seeds to the saucepan and mix.

_____ 14. Drain water from the broccoli.

_____ 15. Pour sauce over the broccoli. Serve hot.

Stuffed Tomatoes

SHOPPING LIST

(4 students per group)	16 students	20 students	24 students	28 students	32 students
tomatoes	16	20	24	28	32
frozen corn	4 cups	5 cups	6 cups	7 cups	8 cups
dried parsley	3 tsp	$3\frac{3}{4}$ tsp	$4\frac{1}{2}$ tsp	$5\frac{1}{4}$ tsp	6 tsp
dried basil	3 tsp	$3\frac{3}{4}$ tsp	$4\frac{1}{2}$ tsp	$5\frac{1}{4}$ tsp	6 tsp

A suggested division of responsibilities

Student A: steps 1, 7

Student B: steps 4, 8

Student C: steps 5, 11

Student D: step 6

All students take part in steps 2, 3, 9, 10

Before class

1. Provide each group with 4 tomatoes.

2. Divide corn into 1-cup packages and give a package to each group.

NOTES

1. Students can measure parsley and basil from the original containers.

2. If desired, crushed potato chips or croutons can be sprinkled over stuffed tomatoes before they are baked.

Stuffed Tomatoes

Makes 4 Servings

Directions

Ingredients	

4 large tomatoes

1 cup frozen corn

$\frac{3}{4}$ **tsp dried parsley**

$\frac{3}{4}$ **tsp dried basil**

Utensils

sharp knife

spoon

cutting board

small bowl

measuring cup

measuring spoons

baking pan

_____ 1. Preheat oven to 400°.

_____ 3. Cut top off each **tomato**.

_____ 3. Scoop out the seeds and juice, leaving the tomatoes still whole.

_____ 4. Measure $\frac{1}{3}$ cup tomato pulp. Chop finely and put in small bowl.

_____ 5. Measure **1 cup corn** into small bowl.

_____ 6. Measure $\frac{3}{4}$ **tsp parsley** into small bowl.

_____ 7. Measure $\frac{3}{4}$ **tsp basil** into small bowl.

_____ 8. Mix ingredients in small bowl.

_____ 9. Spoon mixture into tomatoes.

_____ 10. Place tomatoes in baking pan.

_____ 11. Bake 8-10 minutes until heated through.

Succotash Deluxe

SHOPPING LIST

(4 students per group)	16 students	20 students	24 students	28 students	32 students
onions	4	5	6	7	8
dried oregano	2 tsp	$2\frac{1}{2}$ tsp	3 tsp	$3\frac{1}{2}$ tsp	4 tsp
vegetable oil	2 oz	$2\frac{1}{2}$ oz	3 oz	$3\frac{1}{2}$ oz	4 oz
whole-kernel corn	4 cups	5 cups	6 cups	7 cups	8 cups
zucchini	4	5	6	7	8
16-oz cans plum tomatoes	4 cans	5 cans	6 cans	7 cans	8 cans
black pepper	4 dashes	5 dashes	6 dashes	7 dashes	8 dashes

A suggested division of responsibilities

Student A: steps 1, 4
Student B: steps 2, 3, 8
Student C: steps 5, 6
Student D: steps 7, 9

Before class

1. Provide each group with an onion.
2. Divide corn into 1-cup packages and give a package to each group.
3. Provide each group with a zucchini.
4. Provide each group with a 16-oz can of plum tomatoes.

NOTE

1. Students can measure oregano, vegetable oil, and black pepper from original containers.

Succotash Deluxe

Makes 4 Servings

Directions

Ingredients

1 medium onion

$\frac{1}{2}$ **tsp dried oregano**

1 tbsp vegetable oil

1 cup whole-kernel corn

1 small zucchini

1 16-oz can plum tomatoes

dash black pepper

_____ 1. Peel **onion**. Slice and put in saucepan.

_____ 2. Measure $\frac{1}{2}$ **tsp oregano** into saucepan.

_____ 3. Add **1 tbsp vegetable oil** to saucepan.

_____ 4. Cook over medium heat, stirring constantly, until onion is softened.

_____ 5. Measure **1 cup whole-kernel corn** into saucepan.

_____ 6. Trim ends from **zucchini**. Cut into quarters lengthwise, then slice. Add to saucepan.

_____ 7. Drain **tomatoes**. Cut tomatoes into small pieces and add to saucepan.

_____ 8. Sprinkle mixture with **black pepper**.

_____ 9. Stir the ingredients gently. Cook over low heat 10-15 minutes.

Utensils

cutting board

paring knife

saucepan

measuring spoons

wooden spoon

can opener

measuring cup

Vegetable Pickles

SHOPPING LIST

(4 students per group)	16 students	20 students	24 students	28 students	32 students
green onions	4 bunches	5 bunches	6 bunches	7 bunches	8 bunches
sweet red peppers	4	5	6	7	8
zucchini	4	5	6	7	8
carrots	8	10	12	14	16
cucumbers	4	5	6	7	8
distilled white vinegar	24 oz	30 oz	36 oz	42 oz	48 oz
sugar	$\frac{1}{2}$ cup	10 tbsp	$\frac{3}{4}$ cup	14 tbsp	1 cup
fresh ginger root	1″	$1\frac{1}{4}$″	$1\frac{1}{2}$″	$1\frac{3}{4}$″	2″
crushed red pepper	4 pinches	5 pinches	6 pinches	7 pinches	8 pinches

A suggested division of responsibilities

    Student A: steps 1, 4

    Student B: steps 2, 5

    Student C: steps 3, 6

    Student D: steps 8, 9, 10, 11, 12, 13

    All students take part in steps 7, 14, 15, 16, 17

Before class

1. Provide each group with a bunch of green onions.
2. Provide each group with a sweet red pepper.
3. Provide each group with a zucchini.
4. Provide each group with 2 carrots.
5. Cut ginger root into $\frac{1}{4}$″ chunks and give a piece to each group.

NOTES

1. Students can measure water, vinegar, sugar, and crushed red pepper from the original containers.
2. It is not necessary to have canning jars. Old peanut butter jars or other recycled jars will work perfectly.
3. Pickles will be best if allowed to set several days to let the flavors develop.
4. Since the pickles are not actually processed, they will need to be kept refrigerated.
5. The pickles can be saved to use with a main dish served at a school dinner, or donated to a home-economics fund raiser.

Vegetable Pickles

Makes 4 Half-Pint Jars

Directions

Ingredients
1 bunch green onions
1 sweet red pepper
1 medium zucchini
2 carrots
1 cucumber
1 cup water
$\frac{3}{4}$ **cup distilled white vinegar**
2 tbsp sugar
2 slices fresh ginger root
pinch crushed red pepper

_____ 1. Trim **green onions.** Cut into strips $\frac{1}{2}''$ shorter than your jars.

_____ 2. Remove seeds from **sweet red pepper.** Cut into strips $\frac{1}{2}''$ shorter than your jars.

_____ 3. Cut **zucchini** into thin strips $\frac{1}{2}''$ shorter than your jars.

_____ 4. Peel **carrots.** Trim ends. Cut into thin strips $\frac{1}{2}''$ shorter than your jars.

_____ 5. Cut ends off **cucumber.** Cut into thin strips $\frac{1}{2}''$ shorter than your jars.

_____ 6. Rinse jars in very hot water.

_____ 7. Pack a colorful variety of vegetables vertically into the 4 jars.

_____ 8. Measure **1 cup water** into saucepan.

_____ 9. Measure $\frac{3}{4}$ **cup white vinegar** into saucepan.

_____ 10. Cut **2 slices** ($\frac{1}{8}''$ thick) **ginger root.**

_____ 11. Measure **2 tbsp sugar** into the saucepan.

_____ 12. Add a pinch of **crushed red pepper** to the saucepan.

_____ 13. Bring water-vinegar mixture to a boil. Boil 3 minutes.

_____ 14. Strain liquid into the jars of vegetables. Liquid should cover the vegetables.

_____ 15. Let cool about 10 minutes.

_____ 16. Screw tops on tightly. Refrigerate for at least one day to let flavors develop.

_____ 17. Pickles can be stored in the refrigerator up to three weeks.

Utensils

4 half-pint jars with covers
paring knife
cutting board
vegetable peeler
saucepan
measuring cup
measuring spoon
strainer

Zucchini Oregano

SHOPPING LIST

(4 students per group)	16 students	20 students	24 students	28 students	32 students
zucchini	8	10	12	14	16
green onions	8	10	12	14	16
lemons	1	$1\frac{1}{4}$	$1\frac{1}{2}$	$1\frac{3}{4}$	2
dried oregano	2 tsp	$2\frac{1}{2}$ tsp	3 tsp	$3\frac{1}{2}$ tsp	4 tsp
black pepper	4 dashes	5 dashes	6 dashes	7 dashes	8 dashes
small tomatoes	8	10	12	14	16

A suggested division of responsibilities

Student A: steps 1, 4

Student B: steps 2, 5

Student C: steps 3, 6, 7

Student D: steps 8, 9, 10, 11

Before class

1. Provide each group with 2 zucchini.

2. Provide each group with 2 green onions.

3. Cut lemons in quarters and give a piece to each group.

4. Provide each group with 2 small tomatoes.

NOTE

1. Students can measure water, oregano, and black pepper from the original containers.

Zucchini Oregano

Makes 4 Servings

Directions

Ingredients

2 small zucchini

2 green onions

$\frac{1}{4}$ **lemon**

2 tbsp water

$\frac{1}{2}$ **tsp dried oregano**

dash black pepper

2 small tomatoes

Utensils

cutting board
paring knife
skillet with cover
measuring spoons
wooden spoon

_____ 1. Trim ends off **zucchini**. Slice zucchini and put in skillet.

_____ 2. Trim **green onions**. Chop and put in skillet.

_____ 3. Squeeze juice of $\frac{1}{4}$ **lemon** into skillet.

_____ 4. Measure **2 tbsp water** into skillet.

_____ 5. Measure $\frac{1}{2}$ **tsp oregano** into skillet.

_____ 6. Sprinkle **dash of black pepper** over skillet.

_____ 7. Cook over medium-high heat, stirring constantly, about 5 minutes until zucchini is crisp-tender.

_____ 8. Cut **tomatoes** in quarters. Remove core. Slice tomatoes into thin wedges.

_____ 9. Add tomatoes to skillet.

_____ 10. Cover skillet and cook 1 minute longer, just until tomatoes are warmed through.

_____ 11. Serve hot.

Salad Dressings and Dips

Salads to Use with Dressing Recipes

Choose one of these salads to use with your students when they try the salad dressing recipes on pages 144, 146, 154, or 156.

Tossed Salad Bar

	16 students	20 students	24 students	28 students	32 students
lettuce	2 heads	$2\frac{1}{2}$ heads	3 heads	$3\frac{1}{2}$ heads	4 heads
tomatoes	2	$2\frac{1}{2}$	3	$3\frac{1}{2}$	4
cucumbers	2	$2\frac{1}{2}$	3	$3\frac{1}{2}$	4
green peppers	2	$2\frac{1}{2}$	3	$3\frac{1}{2}$	4
carrots	4	5	6	7	8
celery stalks	4	5	6	7	8
garbanzo beans	16 oz	20 oz	24 oz	28 oz	32 oz
croutons	2 oz	$2\frac{1}{2}$ oz	3 oz	$3\frac{1}{2}$ oz	4 oz
bacon bits	4 oz	5 oz	6 oz	7 oz	8 oz

Wash vegetables. Chop each ingredient and put in separate bowls. Students can select from the salad bar and make their own salads.

Salad Platter

	16 students	20 students	24 students	28 students	32 students
leaf lettuce	2 heads	$2\frac{1}{2}$ heads	3 heads	$3\frac{1}{2}$ heads	4 heads
tomatoes	2	$2\frac{1}{2}$	3	$3\frac{1}{2}$	4
mushrooms	8	10	12	14	16
carrots	4	5	6	7	8
scallions	4	5	6	7	8
zucchini	2	$2\frac{1}{2}$	3	$3\frac{1}{2}$	4
green beans	$\frac{1}{2}$ lb	$\frac{5}{8}$ lb	$\frac{3}{4}$ lb	$\frac{7}{8}$ lb	1 lb
hard-boiled eggs	8	10	12	14	16
radishes	8	10	12	14	16

Wash vegetables. Cook eggs. Line a large shallow salad bowl or tray with lettuce. Slice salad ingredients and arrange attractively on lettuce bed.

Dippers to Use with Dip Recipes

The following are sample dippers to use with your class when they try the dip recipes on pages 148, 150, or 152.

Raw Vegetables
  Carrot sticks
  Cauliflower
  Celery sticks
  Broccoli
  Green beans

Baked Potato Chips (see page 110)

Pita Bread
  Cut whole-wheat pitas into wedges.
  If desired, toast pitas before cutting.

Tortilla Chips
  Cut tortillas and bake in 400° oven 8-10 minutes until crisp.
  Warm chips can be sprinkled with mild chili powder.

Cucumber-Herb Dressing

SHOPPING LIST

(4 students per group)	16 students	20 students	24 students	28 students	32 students
cucumbers	4	5	6	7	8
fresh parsley	20-24 stems	25-30 stems	30-36 stems	35-42 stems	40-48 stems
fresh dill	4 stems	5 stems	6 stems	7 stems	8 stems
fresh tarragon	4 stems	5 stems	6 stems	7 stems	8 stems
honey	1 tsp	$1\frac{1}{4}$ tsp	$1\frac{1}{2}$ tsp	$1\frac{3}{4}$ tsp	2 tsp
garlic	4 cloves	5 cloves	6 cloves	7 cloves	8 cloves
green onions	8	10	12	14	16
white wine vinegar	2 tbsp	$7\frac{1}{2}$ tsp	3 tbsp	$10\frac{1}{2}$ tsp	4 tbsp
plain low-fat yogurt	8 oz	10 oz	12 oz	14 oz	16 oz
Dijon mustard	1 tsp	$1\frac{1}{4}$ tsp	$1\frac{1}{2}$ tsp	$1\frac{3}{4}$ tsp	2 tsp

A suggested division of responsibilities

Student A: steps 1, 5, 9, 13
Student B: steps 2, 6, 10, 14
Student C: steps 3, 7, 11
Student D: steps 4, 8, 12

NOTES

1. Students can measure honey, vinegar, yogurt, and mustard from the original containers.

2. Sample salads to use with this dressing are listed on pages 142 and 143.

Before class

1. Provide each group with a cucumber.

2. Provide each group with 5-6 stems fresh parsley.

3. Provide each group with a stem of fresh dill.

4. Provide each group with a stem of fresh tarragon.

5. Provide each group with a clove of garlic.

6. Provide each group with 2 green onions.

Cucumber-Herb Dressing

Makes $\frac{3}{4}$ Cup Dressing

Directions

	Ingredients

1 medium cucumber

5-6 stems fresh parsley

1 stem fresh dill

1 stem fresh tarragon

$\frac{1}{4}$ tsp honey

1 small clove garlic

2 green onions

$1\frac{1}{2}$ tsp white wine vinegar

$\frac{1}{4}$ cup plain low-fat yogurt

$\frac{1}{4}$ tsp Dijon mustard

Utensils

cutting board
paring knife
measuring cup
measuring spoons
blender
garlic press
spoon
small bowl

_____ 1. Peel **cucumber**. Scrape seeds out of the cucumber. Chop cucumber and put in the blender.

_____ 2. Chop parsley. Measure $\frac{1}{2}$ **cup chopped parsley** into the blender.

_____ 3. Chop dill. Measure **1 tbsp chopped dill** into the blender.

_____ 4. Chop tarragon. Measure **1 tsp chopped tarragon** into the blender.

_____ 5. Measure $\frac{1}{4}$ **tsp honey** into the blender.

_____ 6. Peel **garlic**. Crush and add to the blender.

_____ 7. Trim **2 green onions**. Cut into small pieces and add to blender.

_____ 8. Measure $1\frac{1}{2}$ **tsp white wine vinegar** into blender.

_____ 9. Cover blender and blend until smooth.

_____ 10. Pour blended mixture into bowl.

_____ 11. Measure $\frac{1}{4}$ **cup yogurt** into the bowl.

_____ 12. Measure $\frac{1}{4}$ **tsp Dijon mustard** into the bowl.

_____ 13. Stir all ingredients well.

_____ 14. Serve chilled.

French Dressing

SHOPPING LIST

(4 students per group)	16 students	20 students	24 students	28 students	32 students
plain low-fat yogurt	$1\frac{1}{3}$ cups	$1\frac{2}{3}$ cups	2 cups	$2\frac{1}{3}$ cups	$2\frac{2}{3}$ cups
catsup	4 oz	5 oz	6 oz	7 oz	8 oz
cider vinegar	2 oz	$2\frac{1}{2}$ oz	3 oz	$3\frac{1}{2}$ oz	4 oz
reduced-calorie mayonnaise	8 tsp	10 tsp	4 tbsp	14 tsp	16 tsp
garlic	4 cloves	5 cloves	6 cloves	7 cloves	8 cloves
honey	1 tsp	$1\frac{1}{4}$ tsp	$1\frac{1}{2}$ tsp	$1\frac{3}{4}$ tsp	2 tsp
black pepper	4 dashes	5 dashes	6 dashes	7 dashes	8 dashes

A suggested division of responsibilities

Student A: steps 1, 4, 9
Student B: steps 2, 5, 10
Student C: steps 3, 7
Student D: steps 6, 8

Before class

1. Provide each group with a garlic clove.

NOTES

1. Students can measure yogurt, catsup, water, vinegar, mayonnaise, honey, and black pepper from the original containers.

2. Sample salads to use with this dressing are listed on pages 142 and 143.

French Dressing

Makes $\frac{1}{2}$ Cup Dressing

Directions

Ingredients

$\frac{1}{3}$ **cup plain low-fat yogurt**

2 tbsp catsup

1 tbsp water

1 tbsp cider vinegar

2 tsp reduced-calorie mayonnaise

1 clove garlic

$\frac{1}{4}$ **tsp honey**

dash black pepper

_____ 1. Measure $\frac{1}{3}$ **cup yogurt** into the blender.

_____ 2. Measure **2 tbsp catsup** into the blender.

_____ 3. Measure **1 tbsp water** into the blender.

_____ 4. Measure **1 tbsp cider vinegar** into the blender.

_____ 5. Measure **2 tsp reduced-calorie mayonnaise** into the blender.

_____ 6. Peel **garlic clove**. Crush and add to blender.

_____ 7. Measure $\frac{1}{4}$ **tsp honey** into blender.

_____ 8. Add a **dash of black pepper** to the blender.

_____ 9. Put cover on blender. Blend until ingredients are thoroughly mixed.

_____ 10. Store in covered jar in the refrigerator.

Utensils

blender
measuring cup
measuring spoons
garlic press
covered jar

Light and Tasty Cooking Labs

Onion Dip

SHOPPING LIST

(4 students per group)	16 students	20 students	24 students	28 students	32 students
low-fat cottage cheese	16 oz	20 oz	24 oz	28 oz	32 oz
low-fat yogurt	16 oz	20 oz	24 oz	28 oz	32 oz
dry onion-soup mix	2 envelopes	$2\frac{1}{2}$ envelopes	3 envelopes	$3\frac{1}{2}$ envelopes	4 envelopes

A suggested division of responsibilities

Student A: step 1
Student B: steps 2, 3
Student C: steps 4, 6
Student D: steps 5, 7

Before class

1. Split envelopes of dry onion-soup mix. Be sure to mix seasonings so each package contains equal amounts of all ingredients.

NOTES

1. Students can measure cottage cheese and yogurt from original containers.

2. Dippers to use with this dip recipe are listed on **page 143**.

Onion Dip

Makes 1 Cup Dip

Directions

Ingredients
$\frac{1}{2}$ cup low-fat cottage cheese
$\frac{1}{2}$ cup plain low-fat yogurt
$\frac{1}{2}$ envelope dry onion-soup mix

Utensils

measuring cup

blender

small bowl

mixing spoon

_____ 1. Measure $\frac{1}{2}$ cup **cottage cheese** into blender.

_____ 2. Cover and blend cottage cheese until smooth.

_____ 3. Spoon blended cottage cheese into bowl.

_____ 4. Measure $\frac{1}{2}$ cup **yogurt** into bowl.

_____ 5. Add $\frac{1}{2}$ **envelope dry onion-soup mix** to bowl.

_____ 6. Mix all ingredients.

_____ 7. Served chilled with a variety of raw vegetables to use as dippers.

Salsa

SHOPPING LIST

(4 students per group)	16 students	20 students	24 students	28 students	32 students
large tomatoes	4	5	6	7	8
small onions	2	$2\frac{1}{2}$	3	$3\frac{1}{2}$	4
green onions	4	5	6	7	8
chili peppers	4	5	6	7	8
garlic	4 cloves	5 cloves	6 cloves	7 cloves	8 cloves
limes	1	$1\frac{1}{4}$	$1\frac{1}{2}$	$1\frac{3}{4}$	2

A suggested division of responsibilities

Student A: steps 1, 8

Student B: steps 2, 5

Student C: steps 3, 6

Student D: steps 4, 7

NOTE

1. Sample dippers to use with this dip recipe are listed on page 143.

Before class

1. Provide each group with a tomato.
2. Cut onions in half and give one piece to each group.
3. Provide each group with a green onion.
4. Provide each group with a chili pepper.
5. Provide each group with a garlic clove.
6. Cut limes in quarters and give a piece to each group.

Salsa

Makes $\frac{3}{4}$ Cup

Directions

Ingredients

1 large tomato

$\frac{1}{2}$ **small onion**

1 green onion

1 green chili pepper (fresh or canned)

1 small clove garlic

$\frac{1}{4}$ **lime**

_____ 1. Remove core from **tomato**. Chop tomato and place in bowl.

_____ 2. Peel $\frac{1}{2}$ **small onion**. Chop onion finely and add to bowl.

_____ 3. Trim **green onion**. Chop finely and add to bowl.

_____ 4. Remove stem and seeds from **chili pepper**. Chop very finely and add to bowl.

_____ 5. Peel **garlic clove**. Crush and add to bowl.

_____ 6. Squeeze juice of $\frac{1}{4}$ **lime** into the bowl.

_____ 7. Mix all ingredients together.

_____ 8. Serve chilled as a dip or as a condiment for eggs or sandwiches.

Utensils

paring knife

cutting board

small bowl

mixing spoon

garlic press

Spaghetti Dip

SHOPPING LIST

(4 students per group)	16 students	20 students	24 students	28 students	32 students
low-fat cottage cheese	32 oz	40 oz	48 oz	56 oz	64 oz
buttermilk	$\frac{1}{2}$ cup	10 tbsp	$\frac{3}{4}$ cup	14 tbsp	1 cup
lemons	1	$1\frac{1}{4}$	$1\frac{1}{2}$	$1\frac{3}{4}$	2
dry spaghetti-sauce mix	$\frac{1}{2}$ cup	10 tbsp	$\frac{3}{4}$ cup	14 tbsp	1 cup
green peppers	4	5	6	7	8

A suggested division of responsibilities

Student A: steps 1, 8, 9
Student B: steps 2, 5
Student C: steps 3, 6
Student D: steps 4, 7

Before class

1. Cut lemons in quarters and give each group a piece.

2. Provide each group with a green pepper.

NOTES

1. Students can measure cottage cheese, buttermilk, and spaghetti-sauce mix from the original containers.

2. Sample dippers to use with this dip recipe are listed on **page 143**.

Spaghetti Dip

Makes 1 Cup Dip

Directions

Ingredients

1 cup low-fat cottage cheese

2 tbsp buttermilk

$\frac{1}{4}$ **lemon**

**2 tbsp dry spaghetti-
sauce mix**

1 large green pepper

Utensils

blender
measuring cup
measuring spoons
sharp knife

_____ 1. Measure **1 cup cottage cheese** into the blender.

_____ 2. Measure **2 tbsp buttermilk** into the blender.

_____ 3. Squeeze the juice of $\frac{1}{4}$ **lemon** into the blender.

_____ 4. Cover blender. Blend until smooth.

_____ 5. Measure **2 tbsp dry spaghetti-sauce mix** into the blender.

_____ 6. Slice the top off the **green pepper**. Set aside the main part of the green pepper.

_____ 7. Remove the core and seeds from the green pepper top. Add the green pepper top to the blender.

_____ 8. Cover blender and blend just until green pepper is coarsely chopped and the sauce mix is blended.

_____ 9. Use the green pepper as a serving dish for the dip.

Thousand-Island Dressing

SHOPPING LIST

(4 students per group)	16 students	20 students	24 students	28 students	32 students
eggs	4	5	6	7	8
plain low-fat yogurt	32 oz	40 oz	48 oz	56 oz	64 oz
catsup	6 oz	$7\frac{1}{2}$ oz	9 oz	$10\frac{1}{2}$ oz	12 oz
dill pickle slices	16-20	20-25	24-30	28-35	32-40
black pepper	4 dashes	5 dashes	6 dashes	7 dashes	8 dashes

A suggested division of responsibilities

    Student A: steps 1, 2, 3, 4, 6

    Student B: steps 5, 9

    Student C: steps 7, 10

    Student D: steps 8, 11

Before class

1. Provide each group with an egg.
2. Provide each group with 4-5 dill pickle slices.

NOTES

1. Students can measure yogurt, catsup, and black pepper from the original containers.
2. Sample salads to use with this dressing are listed on pages 142 and 143.

Thousand-Island Dressing

Makes 1 Cup Dressing

Directions

Ingredients

1 egg

1 cup plain low-fat yogurt

3 tbsp catsup

4-5 dill pickle slices

black pepper

Utensils

saucepan with cover

measuring cup

measuring spoons

small bowl

paring knife

cutting board

mixing spoon

_____ 1. Place **egg** in saucepan. Cover with warm water.

_____ 2. Heat water to boiling, then remove saucepan from heat and cover tightly.

_____ 3. Let egg stand in hot water for 15 minutes. Drain. Rinse in cold water.

_____ 4. Peel egg and chop into fine pieces.

_____ 5. Measure **1 cup yogurt** into small bowl.

_____ 6. Add chopped egg.

_____ 7. Chop **dill pickles** into tiny pieces. Add to bowl.

_____ 8. Measure **3 tbsp catsup** into bowl.

_____ 9. Sprinkle with **black pepper**.

_____ 10. Mix well.

_____ 11. Stored in a covered jar, this dressing will keep in the refrigerator for a week.

Vinaigrette Dressing

SHOPPING LIST

(4 students per group)	16 students	20 students	24 students	28 students	32 students
white vinegar	4 oz	5 oz	6 oz	7 oz	8 oz
pineapple juice (unsweetened)	16 oz	20 oz	24 oz	28 oz	32 oz
lemons	1	$1\frac{1}{4}$	$1\frac{1}{2}$	$1\frac{3}{4}$	2
dry mustard	$\frac{1}{2}$ tsp	$\frac{5}{8}$ tsp	$\frac{3}{4}$ tsp	$\frac{7}{8}$ tsp	1 tsp
garlic	4 cloves	5 cloves	6 cloves	7 cloves	8 cloves
celery	2 stalks	$2\frac{1}{2}$ stalks	3 stalks	$3\frac{1}{2}$ stalks	4 stalks
green onions	4	5	6	7	8
red sweet pepper	1	$1\frac{1}{4}$	$1\frac{1}{2}$	$1\frac{3}{4}$	2

A suggested division of responsibilities

Student A: steps 1, 5, 9
Student B: steps 2, 6, 10
Student C: steps 3, 7
Student D: steps 4, 8

Before class

1. Cut lemons in quarters and give a piece to each group.
2. Provide each group with a garlic clove.
3. Cut celery stalks in half and give each group a piece.
4. Provide each group with a green onion.
5. Cut red peppers in quarters and give each group a piece.

NOTES

1. Students can measure vinegar, pineapple juice, and dry mustard from the original containers.
2. Sample salads to use with this dressing are listed on page 142 and 143.

Vinaigrette Dressing

Makes 1 Cup Dressing

Directions

Ingredients

2 tbsp white vinegar

$\frac{1}{2}$ **cup unsweetened pineapple juice**

$\frac{1}{4}$ **lemon**

$\frac{1}{8}$ **tsp dry mustard**

1 clove garlic

$\frac{1}{2}$ **stalk celery**

1 green onion

$\frac{1}{4}$ **red sweet pepper**

_____ 1. Measure **2 tbsp white vinegar** into blender.

_____ 2. Measure $\frac{1}{2}$ **cup unsweetened pineapple juice** into blender.

_____ 3. Squeeze **juice of** $\frac{1}{4}$ **lemon** into blender.

_____ 4. Measure $\frac{1}{8}$ **tsp dry mustard** into blender.

_____ 5. Peel **garlic**. Add to blender.

_____ 6. Trim **celery**. Cut into 3 or 4 pieces and add to blender.

_____ 7. Trim **green onion**. Cut into 3 or 4 pieces and add to blender.

_____ 8. Remove seeds and stem from **red sweet pepper**. Cut pepper into 3 or 4 pieces and add to blender.

_____ 9. Cover blender. Blend until ingredients are mixed.

_____ 10. Dressing may be stored for a few days in a covered container in the refrigerator.

Utensils

blender
measuring spoons
measuring cup
sharp knife
cutting board

Breads

Apple Muffins

SHOPPING LIST

(4 students per group)	16 students	20 students	24 students	28 students	32 students
whole-wheat flour	$2\frac{2}{3}$ cups	$3\frac{1}{3}$ cups	4 cups	$4\frac{2}{3}$ cups	$5\frac{1}{3}$ cups
baking powder	1 tbsp	$3\frac{3}{4}$ tsp	$4\frac{1}{2}$ tsp	$5\frac{1}{2}$ tsp	2 tbsp
baking soda	$1\frac{1}{2}$ tsp	$\frac{5}{8}$ tsp	$\frac{3}{4}$ tsp	$\frac{7}{8}$ tsp	1 tsp
ground cinnamon	1 tsp	$1\frac{1}{4}$ tsp	$1\frac{1}{2}$ tsp	$1\frac{3}{4}$ tsp	2 tsp
eggs (small)	4	5	6	7	8
vegetable oil	2 oz	$2\frac{1}{2}$ oz	3 oz	$3\frac{1}{2}$ oz	4 oz
apple juice	$1\frac{1}{3}$ cups	$1\frac{2}{3}$ cups	2 cups	$2\frac{1}{3}$ cups	$2\frac{2}{3}$ cups
small apples	4	5	6	7	8
paper liners	16	20	24	28	32

A suggested division of responsibilities

Student A: steps 1, 3, 5, 11, 17

Student B: steps 2, 4, 6, 12, 18

Student C: steps 7, 8, 9, 10, 16

Student D: steps 13, 14, 15

Before class

1. Provide each group with an egg.

2. Provide each group with an apple.

3. Provide each group with 4 paper liners.

NOTE

1. Students can measure flour, baking powder, baking soda, cinnamon, vegetable oil, and apple juice from the original containers.

Apple Muffins

Makes 4 Muffins

Ingredients

$\frac{2}{3}$ cup whole-wheat flour

$\frac{3}{4}$ tsp baking powder

$\frac{1}{8}$ tsp baking soda

$\frac{1}{4}$ tsp cinnamon

1 small egg

1 tbsp vegetable oil

$\frac{1}{3}$ cup apple juice

1 small apple

Utensils

medium bowl

measuring cup

measuring spoons

small bowl

mixing spoon

cutting board

paring knife

muffin pan

4 paper liners

Directions

_____ 1. Preheat oven to 400°.

_____ 2. Measure $\frac{2}{3}$ cup whole-wheat flour into medium bowl.

_____ 3. Measure $\frac{3}{4}$ tsp baking powder into medium bowl.

_____ 4. Measure $\frac{1}{8}$ tsp baking soda into medium bowl.

_____ 5. Measure $\frac{1}{4}$ tsp cinnamon into medium bowl.

_____ 6. Mix dry ingredients.

_____ 7. Break egg into small bowl.

_____ 8. Measure 1 tbsp vegetable oil into small bowl.

_____ 9. Measure $\frac{1}{3}$ cup apple juice into small bowl.

_____ 10. Mix liquid ingredients together.

_____ 11. Add liquid ingredients to dry ingredients.

_____ 12. Stir the mixture until flour is just moistened.

_____ 13. Cut apple into quarters. Remove core.

_____ 14. Chop apple and add to batter.

_____ 15. Mix gently.

_____ 16. Put paper liners in 4 muffin cups.

_____ 17. Divide batter among 4 muffin cups.

_____ 18. Bake 20 minutes.

Applesauce Muffins

SHOPPING LIST

(4 students per group)	16 students	20 students	24 students	28 students	32 students
whole-wheat flour	$1\frac{1}{3}$ cups	$1\frac{2}{3}$ cups	2 cups	$2\frac{1}{3}$ cups	$2\frac{2}{3}$ cups
white flour	$1\frac{1}{3}$ cups	$1\frac{2}{3}$ cups	2 cups	$2\frac{1}{3}$ cups	$2\frac{2}{3}$ cups
baking powder	1 tbsp	$3\frac{3}{4}$ tsp	$4\frac{1}{2}$ tsp	$5\frac{1}{4}$ tsp	2 tbsp
baking soda	1 tsp	$1\frac{1}{4}$ tsp	$1\frac{1}{2}$ tsp	$1\frac{3}{4}$ tsp	2 tsp
ground cinnamon	2 tsp	$2\frac{1}{2}$ tsp	3 tsp	$3\frac{1}{2}$ tsp	4 tsp
ground nutmeg	$\frac{1}{2}$ tsp	$\frac{5}{8}$ tsp	$\frac{3}{4}$ tsp	$\frac{7}{8}$ tsp	1 tsp
raisins	1 cup	$1\frac{1}{4}$ cups	$1\frac{1}{2}$ cups	$1\frac{3}{4}$ cups	2 cups
unsweetened applesauce	$1\frac{1}{3}$ cups	$1\frac{2}{3}$ cups	2 cups	$2\frac{1}{3}$ cups	$2\frac{2}{3}$ cups
eggs (small)	4	5	6	7	8
vegetable oil	8 tsp	10 tsp	4 tbsp	14 tsp	16 tsp
paper liners	16	20	24	28	32

A suggested division of responsibilities

    Student A: steps 1, 3, 5, 7, 13

    Student B: steps 2, 4, 6, 8, 14

    Student C: steps 9, 11, 15, 17

    Student D: steps 10, 12, 16

Before class

1. Provide each group with a egg.

2. Divide raisins into $\frac{1}{4}$-cup packets and give a packet to each group.

3. Provide each group with 4 paper liners.

NOTE

1. Students can measure flour, baking powder, baking soda, cinnamon, nutmeg, applesauce, and vegetable oil from the original containers.

Applesauce Muffins

Makes 4 Muffins

Ingredients

$\frac{1}{3}$ cup whole-wheat flour

$\frac{1}{3}$ cup white flour

$\frac{3}{4}$ tsp baking powder

$\frac{1}{4}$ tsp baking soda

$\frac{1}{2}$ tsp cinnamon

$\frac{1}{8}$ tsp nutmeg

$\frac{1}{4}$ cup raisins

$\frac{1}{3}$ cup unsweetened applesauce

1 small egg

2 tsp vegetable oil

Utensils

small bowl

measuring cup

measuring spoons

medium bowl

mixing spoon

muffin pan

4 paper liners

Directions

_____ 1. Preheat oven to 375°.

_____ 2. Measure $\frac{1}{3}$ cup whole-wheat flour into small bowl.

_____ 3. Measure $\frac{1}{3}$ cup white flour into small bowl.

_____ 4. Measure $\frac{3}{4}$ tsp baking powder into small bowl.

_____ 5. Measure $\frac{1}{4}$ tsp baking soda into small bowl.

_____ 6. Measure $\frac{1}{2}$ tsp cinnamon into small bowl.

_____ 7. Measure $\frac{1}{8}$ tsp nutmeg into small bowl.

_____ 8. Measure $\frac{1}{4}$ cup raisins into small bowl.

_____ 9. Measure $\frac{1}{3}$ cup applesauce into medium bowl.

_____ 10. Break egg into bowl with applesauce.

_____ 11. Measure 2 tsp vegetable oil into bowl with applesauce.

_____ 12. Mix applesauce, egg, and oil together.

_____ 13. Mix dry ingredients and add to applesauce mixture.

_____ 14. Stir just until dry ingredients are moistened.

_____ 15. Put paper liners in muffin pan.

_____ 16. Divide batter among 4 muffin cups.

_____ 17. Bake muffins for 20 minutes.

Blueberry Muffins

SHOPPING LIST

(4 students per group)	16 students	20 students	24 students	28 students	32 students
flour	$2\frac{2}{3}$ cups	$3\frac{1}{3}$ cups	4 cups	$4\frac{2}{3}$ cups	$5\frac{1}{3}$ cups
sugar	$\frac{1}{2}$ cup	$\frac{5}{8}$ cup	$\frac{3}{4}$ cup	$\frac{7}{8}$ cup	1 cup
baking powder	4 tsp	5 tsp	2 tbsp	7 tsp	8 tsp
ground cinnamon	$\frac{1}{2}$ tsp	$\frac{5}{8}$ tsp	$\frac{3}{4}$ tsp	$\frac{7}{8}$ tsp	1 tsp
ground nutmeg	$\frac{1}{2}$ tsp	$\frac{5}{8}$ tsp	$\frac{3}{4}$ tsp	$\frac{7}{8}$ tsp	1 tsp
blueberries, fresh or frozen	$1\frac{1}{3}$ cups	$1\frac{2}{3}$ cups	2 cups	$2\frac{1}{3}$ cups	$2\frac{2}{3}$ cups
eggs (small)	4	5	6	7	8
orange juice	8 oz	10 oz	12 oz	14 oz	16 oz
vegetable oil	$\frac{1}{4}$ cup	5 tbsp	6 tbsp	7 tbsp	$\frac{1}{2}$ cup
paper liners	16	20	24	28	32

A suggested division of responsibilities

Student A: steps 1, 3, 5, 7, 15

Student B: steps 2, 4, 6, 8, 16

Student C: steps 9, 11, 13, 17

Student D: steps 10, 12, 14

Before class

1. Divide blueberries into $\frac{1}{3}$-cup packages and give a package to each group.

2. Provide each group with an egg.

3. Provide each group with 4 paper liners.

NOTE

1. Students can measure flour, sugar, baking powder, cinnamon, nutmeg, orange juice, and vegetable oil from the original containers.

Blueberry Muffins

Makes 4 Muffins

Directions

Ingredients

$\frac{2}{3}$ **cup flour**

2 tbsp sugar

1 tsp baking powder

$\frac{1}{8}$ **tsp cinnamon**

$\frac{1}{8}$ **tsp nutmeg**

$\frac{1}{3}$ **cup blueberries (fresh or frozen)**

1 small egg

$\frac{1}{4}$ **cup orange juice**

1 tbsp vegetable oil

Utensils

medium bowl
measuring cup
measuring spoons
mixing spoon
small bowl
muffin pan
4 paper liners

_____ 1. Preheat oven to 400°.

_____ 2. Measure $\frac{2}{3}$ **cup flour** into medium bowl.

_____ 3. Measure **2 tbsp sugar** into medium bowl.

_____ 4. Measure **1 tsp baking powder** into medium bowl.

_____ 5. Measure $\frac{1}{8}$ **tsp cinnamon** into medium bowl.

_____ 6. Measure $\frac{1}{8}$ **tsp nutmeg** into medium bowl.

_____ 7. Mix dry ingredients well.

_____ 8. Measure $\frac{1}{3}$ **cup blueberries** into dry ingredients.

_____ 9. Break **egg** into small bowl.

_____ 10. Measure $\frac{1}{3}$ **cup orange juice** into small bowl.

_____ 11. Measure **1 tbsp vegetable oil** into small bowl.

_____ 12. Mix liquid ingredients.

_____ 13. Pour liquid ingredients into dry ingredients.

_____ 14. Stir gently, just until ingredients are blended.

_____ 15. Put paper liners in 4 muffin cups.

_____ 16. Divide batter among 4 muffin cups.

_____ 17. Bake 20-25 minutes.

Bran Muffins

SHOPPING LIST

(4 students per group)	16 students	20 students	24 students	28 students	32 students
bran cereal	2 cups	$2\frac{1}{2}$ cups	3 cups	$3\frac{1}{2}$ cups	4 cups
skim milk	1 cup	$1\frac{1}{4}$ cups	$1\frac{1}{2}$ cups	$1\frac{3}{4}$ cups	2 cups
vegetable oil	2 oz	$2\frac{1}{2}$ oz	3 oz	$3\frac{1}{2}$ oz	4 oz
honey	4 oz	5 oz	6 oz	7 oz	8 oz
eggs (small)	4	5	6	7	8
flour	$1\frac{1}{3}$ cups	$1\frac{2}{3}$ cups	2 cups	$2\frac{1}{3}$ cups	$2\frac{2}{3}$ cups
baking powder	4 tsp	5 tsp	6 tsp	7 tsp	8 tsp
paper liners	16	20	24	28	32

A suggested division of responsibilities

Student A: steps 1, 3, 5, 7

Student B: steps 2, 4, 6, 13

Student C: steps 8, 10, 12

Student D: steps 9, 11, 14, 15

NOTES

1. Students can measure milk, vegetable oil, honey, flour, and baking powder from the original containers.

2. Raisins or dates could be added to this recipe as a variation.

Before class

1. Divide bran cereal into $\frac{1}{2}$-cup packages and give a package to each group. (If using a cereal such as *All-Bran*, measure it just as it comes from the box. If using something like *Bran Flakes* or *Corn Bran*, crush the cereal before measuring.)

2. Provide each group with an egg.

3. Provide each group with 4 paper liners.

Bran Muffins

Makes 4 Muffins

Directions

Ingredients

$\frac{1}{2}$ **cup bran cereal**

$\frac{1}{4}$ **cup skim milk**

1 tbsp vegetable oil

2 tbsp honey

1 small egg

$\frac{1}{3}$ **cup flour**

1 tsp baking powder

Utensils

2 bowls
measuring cup
measuring spoons
fork
muffin tin
4 paper liners

_____ 1. Preheat oven to 400°.

_____ 2. Measure $\frac{1}{2}$ **cup bran cereal** into a bowl. (If you are using flakes, crush them before measuring.)

_____ 3. Measure $\frac{1}{4}$ **cup skim milk** into the bowl.

_____ 4. Measure **1 tbsp vegetable oil** into the bowl.

_____ 5. Measure **2 tbsp honey** into the bowl.

_____ 6. Break **egg** into the bowl.

_____ 7. Mix all the ingredients in the first bowl.

_____ 8. Measure $\frac{1}{3}$ **cup flour** into the second bowl.

_____ 9. Measure **1 tsp baking powder** into the bowl with the flour.

_____ 10. Use a fork to mix the flour and the baking powder together.

_____ 11. Add the flour mixture to the first bowl.

_____ 12. Using a fork, gently stir the ingredients, just until the flour is wet.

_____ 13. Put paper liners in the muffin tin.

_____ 14. Divide the batter into 4 muffin cups.

_____ 15. Bake about 20 minutes until browned on top.

Cottage-Cheese Biscuits

SHOPPING LIST

(4 students per group)	16 students	20 students	24 students	28 students	32 students
whole-wheat flour	$1\frac{1}{3}$ cups	$1\frac{2}{3}$ cups	2 cups	$2\frac{1}{3}$ cups	$2\frac{2}{3}$ cups
white flour	2 cups +	$2\frac{1}{2}$ cups +	3 cups +	$3\frac{1}{2}$ cups +	4 cups +
baking powder	2 tbsp	$7\frac{1}{2}$ tsp	3 tbsp	$10\frac{1}{2}$ tsp	4 tbsp
baking soda	$\frac{1}{2}$ tsp	$\frac{5}{8}$ tsp	$\frac{3}{4}$ tsp	$\frac{7}{8}$ tsp	1 tsp
cream of tartar	$\frac{1}{2}$ tsp	$\frac{5}{8}$ tsp	$\frac{3}{4}$ tsp	$\frac{7}{8}$ tsp	1 tsp
margarine	$\frac{1}{2}$ stick	5 tbsp	6 tbsp	7 tbsp	1 stick
honey	2 oz	$2\frac{1}{2}$ oz	3 oz	$3\frac{1}{2}$ oz	4 oz
low-fat cottage cheese	16 oz	20 oz	24 oz	28 oz	32 oz

A suggested division of responsibilities

Student A: steps 1, 3, 5, 7, 16

Student B: steps 2, 4, 6, 8, 9, 17

Student C: steps 10, 12, 14, 18

Student D: steps 11, 13, 15, 19, 20

Before class

1. Divide margarine into 1-tbsp chunks and give a piece to each group.

NOTE

1. Students can measure flours, baking powder, baking soda, cream of tartar, honey, water, and cottage cheese from original containers.

Cottage-Cheese Bicuits

Makes 4 Biscuits

Directions

Ingredients

$\frac{1}{3}$ **cup whole-wheat flour**

$\frac{1}{2}$ **cup white flour**

$1\frac{1}{2}$ **tsp baking powder**

$\frac{1}{8}$ **tsp baking soda**

$\frac{1}{8}$ **tsp cream of tartar**

1 tbsp margarine

1 tbsp honey

1 tbsp water

$\frac{1}{2}$ **cup low-fat cottage cheese**

additional flour

Utensils

medium bowl
measuring cup
measuring spoons
small bowl
fork
knife
baking sheet

_____ 1. Preheat oven to 425°.

_____ 2. Measure $\frac{1}{3}$ **cup whole-wheat flour** into medium bowl.

_____ 3. Measure $\frac{1}{2}$ **cup white flour** into medium bowl.

_____ 4. Measure $1\frac{1}{2}$ **tsp baking powder** into medium bowl.

_____ 5. Measure $\frac{1}{8}$ **tsp baking soda** into medium bowl.

_____ 6. Measure $\frac{1}{8}$ **tsp cream of tartar** into medium bowl.

_____ 7. Use fork to mix dry ingredients.

_____ 8. Add **1 tbsp margarine** to dry ingredients.

_____ 9. Use fingers to mix margarine into dry ingredients.

_____ 10. Measure **1 tbsp honey** into small bowl.

_____ 11. Measure **1 tbsp water** into small bowl.

_____ 12. Mix honey and water.

_____ 13. Measure $\frac{1}{2}$ **cup cottage cheese** into bowl with honey.

_____ 14. Mix cottage cheese with honey and water.

_____ 15. Add cottage-cheese mixture to dry ingredients.

_____ 16. Mix thoroughly.

_____ 17. Turn dough onto floured surface and knead dough 1 or 2 minutes.

_____ 18. Shape dough into a fat roll about 4″ long.

_____ 19. Cut into 4 slices and place on baking sheet.

_____ 20. Bake 10-12 minutes until lightly browned.

Irish Soda Bread

SHOPPING LIST

(4 students per group)	16 students	20 students	24 students	28 students	32 students
flour	16 cups +	20 cups +	24 cups +	28 cups +	32 cups +
salt	2 tsp	$2\frac{1}{2}$ tsp	3 tsp	$3\frac{1}{2}$ tsp	4 tsp
baking soda	4 tsp	5 tsp	6 tsp	7 tsp	8 tsp
buttermilk	1 qt	5 cups	$1\frac{1}{2}$ qt	7 cups	2 qt

A suggested division of responsibilities

> Student A: steps 1, 6, 9
> Student B: steps 2, 7, 11
> Student C: steps 3, 8, 10
> Student D: steps 4, 5, 12

NOTES

1. Students can measure all ingredients directly from original containers.

2. As a variation, add $\frac{3}{4}$ cup of raisins to the dry ingredients to make a raisin bread.

3. Make this bread with raisins and then use it for the *Apple-Tuna Toasts* on page 76.

Irish Soda Bread

Makes 1 Loaf

Ingredients

4 cups flour

$\frac{1}{2}$ **tsp salt**

1 tsp baking soda

1 cup buttermilk

additional flour

Utensils

large mixing bowl
measuring cup
measuring spoons
wooden spoon
baking sheet
sharp knife

Directions

_____ 1. Preheat oven to 425°.

_____ 2. Measure **4 cups flour** into the bowl.

_____ 3. Measure $\frac{1}{2}$ **tsp salt** into the bowl.

_____ 4. Measure **1 tsp baking soda** into the bowl.

_____ 5. Use your hands to mix the ingredients together.

_____ 6. Measure **1 cup buttermilk** into the dry ingredients.

_____ 7. Use a spoon to mix into a soft dough.

_____ 8. With your floured hands, gently knead the dough into a ball.

_____ 9. Sprinkle a small amount of **additional flour** on the baking sheet.

_____ 10. Place the dough ball on the baking sheet. Press gently to slightly flatten loaf.

_____ 11. Use the sharp knife to make a cross on the top of the bread.

_____ 12. Bake for 25 to 30 minutes until lightly browned.

Sesame-Oat Crackers

SHOPPING LIST

(4 students per group)	16 students	20 students	24 students	28 students	32 students
rolled oats	2 cups	$2\frac{1}{2}$ cups	3 cups	$3\frac{1}{2}$ cups	4 cups
whole-wheat flour	1 cup +	$1\frac{1}{4}$ cups +	$1\frac{1}{2}$ cups +	$1\frac{3}{4}$ cups +	2 cups +
wheat germ	$\frac{1}{2}$ cup	10 tbsp	$\frac{3}{4}$ cup	14 tbsp	1 cup
sesame seeds	4 tsp	5 tsp	6 tsp	7 tsp	8 tsp
margarine	$\frac{1}{2}$ stick	5 tbsp	6 tbsp	7 tbsp	1 stick
apple juice (unsweetened)	4 oz	5 oz	6 oz	7 oz	8 oz

A suggested division of responsibilities

Student A: steps 1, 7, 11, 12

Student B: steps 2, 3, 4, 15

Student C: steps 5, 8, 13, 14

Student D: steps 6, 9, 10, 16, 17

Before class

1. Measure rolled oats into $\frac{1}{2}$-cup packages and give a package to each group.

2. Divide margarine into 1-tbsp chunks and give a piece to each group.

NOTE

1. Students can measure flour, wheat germ, sesame seeds, and apple juice from the original containers.

Sesame-Oat Crackers

Makes 16 Crackers

Directions

Ingredients

$\frac{1}{2}$ **cup rolled oats**

$\frac{1}{4}$ **cup whole-wheat flour**

2 tbsp wheat germ

1 tsp sesame seeds

1 tbsp margarine

2 tbsp apple juice

_____ 1. Preheat oven to 375°.

_____ 2. Measure $\frac{1}{2}$ **cup rolled oats** into blender.

_____ 3. Cover. Blend until oats are evenly ground.

_____ 4. Pour oats into the bowl.

_____ 5. Measure $\frac{1}{4}$ **cup whole-wheat flour** into the bowl.

_____ 6. Measure **2 tbsp wheat germ** into the bowl.

_____ 7. Measure **1 tsp sesame seeds** into the bowl.

_____ 8. Mix the dry ingredients together.

_____ 9. Measure **1 tbsp margarine** into the bowl.

_____ 10. Use your fingers to mix the margarine into the dry ingredients.

_____ 11. Add **2 tbsp apple juice** to the bowl.

_____ 12. Mix thoroughly.

_____ 13. Use your hands to shape the dough into a ball. If dough is too moist, add a little flour. If dough is too dry, add a few drops of juice.

_____ 14. With rolling pin, roll dough into square 6″ x 6″. Sprinkle lightly with flour if dough sticks to surface.

_____ 15. Cut into 16 squares.

_____ 16. Place crackers on baking sheet.

_____ 17. Bake 10-12 minutes until edges brown.

Utensils

measuring cup
blender
bowl
measuring spoons
mixing spoon
rolling pin
knife
baking sheet

Whole-Wheat Corn Muffins

SHOPPING LIST

(4 students per group)	16 students	20 students	24 students	28 students	32 students
whole-wheat flour	$1\frac{1}{3}$ cups	$1\frac{2}{3}$ cups	2 cups	$2\frac{1}{3}$ cups	$2\frac{2}{3}$ cups
corn meal	1 cup	$1\frac{1}{4}$ cups	$1\frac{1}{2}$ cups	$1\frac{3}{4}$ cups	2 cups
sugar	8 tsp	10 tsp	4 tbsp	14 tsp	16 tsp
baking powder	4 tsp	5 tsp	6 tsp	7 tsp	8 tsp
skim milk	1 cup	$1\frac{1}{4}$ cups	$1\frac{1}{2}$ cups	$1\frac{3}{4}$ cups	2 cups
eggs (small)	4	5	6	7	8
vegetable oil	2 oz	$2\frac{1}{2}$ oz	3 oz	$3\frac{1}{2}$ oz	4 oz
paper liners	16	20	24	28	32

A suggested division of responsibilities

    Student A: steps 1, 3, 5, 13

    Student B: steps 2, 4, 6, 14

    Student C: steps 7, 9, 11

    Student D: steps 8, 10, 12

Before class

1. Provide each group with an egg.

2. Provide each group with 4 paper liners.

NOTE

1. Students can measure flour, corn meal, sugar, baking powder, skim milk, and vegetable oil from the original containers.

Whole-Wheat Corn Muffins

Makes 4 Muffins   **Directions**

Ingredients
$\frac{1}{3}$ cup whole-wheat flour
$\frac{1}{4}$ cup corn meal
2 tsp sugar
1 tsp baking powder
$\frac{1}{4}$ cup skim milk
1 small egg
1 tbsp vegetable oil

_____ 1. Preheat oven to 425°.

_____ 2. Measure $\frac{1}{3}$ cup **whole-wheat flour** into bowl.

_____ 3. Measure $\frac{1}{4}$ cup **corn meal** into bowl.

_____ 4. Measure **2 tsp sugar** into bowl.

_____ 5. Measure **1 tsp baking powder** into bowl.

_____ 6. Use fork to mix dry ingredients.

_____ 7. Measure $\frac{1}{4}$ cup **skim milk** into second bowl.

_____ 8. Add **egg** to milk.

_____ 9. Add **1 tbsp vegetable oil** to milk and egg.

_____ 10. Mix liquid ingredients.

_____ 11. Combine dry and liquid ingredients. Mix with fork just until blended.

_____ 12. Put paper liners in muffin pan.

_____ 13. Fill muffin cups $\frac{2}{3}$ full.

_____ 14. Bake 20 minutes until lightly browned.

Utensils

2 bowls

measuring cup

measuring spoons

fork

muffin pan

4 paper liners

Beverages

Banana Coolers

SHOPPING LIST

(4 students per group)	16 students	20 students	24 students	28 students	32 students
orange juice	8 oz	10 oz	12 oz	14 oz	16 oz
ripe bananas	4	5	6	7	8
skim milk	1 qt	5 cups	6 cups	7 cups	2 qt
honey	2 oz	$2\frac{1}{2}$ oz	3 oz	$3\frac{1}{2}$ oz	4 oz
almond extract	1 tsp	$1\frac{1}{4}$ tsp	$1\frac{1}{2}$ tsp	$1\frac{3}{4}$ tsp	2 tsp
ice cubes	20-24	25-30	30-36	35-42	40-48

A suggested division of responsibilities

Student A: steps 1, 6

Student B: steps 2, 7

Student C: steps 3, 4

Student D: steps 5, 8, 9

All students take part in step 10

Before class

1. Provide each group with a ripe banana.

NOTES

1. Students can measure orange juice, milk, honey, and almond extract from the original containers.

2. Students can get ice cubes from the freezer as needed. If cubes are too big for your blender, put them in a plastic bag and use a hammer to break cubes into smaller pieces.

Banana Coolers

Makes 4 Servings

Directions

Ingredients
$\frac{1}{4}$ cup orange juice
1 ripe banana
1 cup skim milk
1 tbsp honey
$\frac{1}{4}$ tsp almond extract
5 or 6 ice cubes

_____ 1. Put glasses in refrigerator to chill.

_____ 2. Measure $\frac{1}{4}$ **cup orange juice** into blender.

_____ 3. Peel **banana**. Add to blender.

_____ 4. Cover blender and blend banana and orange juice until smooth.

_____ 5. Measure **1 cup skim milk** into blender.

_____ 6. Measure **1 tbsp honey** into blender.

_____ 7. Measure $\frac{1}{4}$ **tsp almond extract** into blender.

_____ 8. Add **5 or 6 ice cubes** to the blender.

_____ 9. Cover blender and blend until smooth.

_____ 10. Pour into chilled glasses and serve immediately.

Utensils

blender
measuring cup
measuring spoons

Cranberry Punch

SHOPPING LIST

(4 students per group)	16 students	20 students	24 students	28 students	32 students
cranberries	$2\frac{2}{3}$ cups	$3\frac{1}{3}$ cups	4 cups	$4\frac{2}{3}$ cups	$5\frac{1}{3}$ cups
apple juice (unsweetened)	48 oz	60 oz	72 oz	84 oz	96 oz
cinnamon sticks	4	5	6	7	8
whole allspice	12	15	18	21	24
club soda	16 oz	20 oz	24 oz	28 oz	32 oz
orange juice	16 oz	20 oz	24 oz	28 oz	32 oz

A suggested division of responsibilities

Student A: steps 1, 8
Student B: steps 2, 7, 9
Student C: steps 3, 6, 10
Student D: steps 4, 5, 11

Before class

1. Divide cranberries into $\frac{2}{3}$-cup packages and give a package to each group.

2. Provide each group with a cinnamon stick.

3. Provide each group with 3 whole allspice.

NOTES

1. Students can measure apple juice, club soda, and orange juice from the original containers.

2. To chill the cranberry liquid more quickly, set the pan in a bowl of ice water.

Cranberry Punch

Makes 4 Servings

Directions

Ingredients

$\frac{2}{3}$ **cup fresh cranberries**

$1\frac{1}{2}$ **cups unsweetened apple juice**

1 stick cinnamon

3 whole allspice

$\frac{1}{2}$ **cup club soda**

$\frac{1}{2}$ **cup orange juice**

Utensils

small saucepan with cover
measuring cup
wooden spoon
strainer
bowl

_____ 1. Wash $\frac{2}{3}$ **cup fresh cranberries**. Discard any that are spoiled. Place cranberries in small saucepan.

_____ 2. Measure $1\frac{1}{2}$ **cups apple juice** into the saucepan.

_____ 3. Add **1 stick cinnamon** to the saucepan.

_____ 4. Add **3 whole allspice**.

_____ 5. Over medium heat, bring cranberry mixture to a boil.

_____ 6. Stir. Cover. Reduce heat and simmer until the berries pop. (About 3 minutes.)

_____ 7. Strain mixture into a bowl. Discard pulp and spices.

_____ 8. Chill cranberry liquid.

_____ 9. Measure $\frac{1}{2}$ **cup club soda** and add to cranberry mixture.

_____ 10. Measure $\frac{1}{2}$ **cup orange juice** and add to cranberry mixture.

_____ 11. Stir punch until blended. Serve immediately over ice.

Hot Tomato Bouillon

SHOPPING LIST

(4 students per group)	16 students	20 students	24 students	28 students	32 students
beef bouillon cubes	8	10	12	14	16
tomato juice	64 oz	80 oz	96 oz	112 oz	128 oz
Worcestershire sauce	4 tsp	5 tsp	6 tsp	7 tsp	8 tsp
hot sauce	8-12 drops	10-15 drops	12-18 drops	14-21 drops	16-24 drops
lemons	2	$2\frac{1}{2}$	3	$3\frac{1}{2}$	4

A suggested division of responsibilities

Student A: steps 1, 5
Student B: steps 2, 3
Student C: steps 4, 6, 7
Student D: steps 8, 9, 10

Before class

1. Provide each group with 2 bouillon cubes.

2. Cut lemons in half and give each group half a lemon.

NOTE

1. Students can measure water, tomato juice, Worcestershire sauce, and hot sauce from the original containers.

Hot Tomato Bouillon

Makes 4 Servings

Directions

Ingredients

2 cups water

2 beef bouillon cubes

2 cups tomato juice

1 tsp Worcestershire sauce

2-3 drops hot sauce

$\frac{1}{2}$ **lemon**

Utensils

saucepan

measuring cup

measuring spoons

wooden spoon

sharp knife

_____ 1. Measure **2 cups water** into a saucepan.

_____ 2. Add **2 bouillon cubes** to the saucepan.

_____ 3. Heat over medium heat, stirring until bouillon is dissolved.

_____ 4. Measure **2 cups tomato juice** into the saucepan.

_____ 5. Measure **1 tsp Worcestershire sauce** into the saucepan.

_____ 6. Add **2-3 drops hot sauce** to the saucepan.

_____ 7. Heat mixture to a boil, stirring occasionally.

_____ 8. Cut 4 slices from the **lemon**.

_____ 9. Place lemon slices in 4 mugs.

_____ 10. Pour hot drink into the mugs.

Iced Apple-Mint Tea

SHOPPING LIST

(4 students per group)	16 students	20 students	24 students	28 students	32 students
orange-pekoe tea bags	12	15	18	21	24
fresh mint leaves	2 cups	$2\frac{1}{2}$ cups	3 cups	$3\frac{1}{2}$ cups	4 cups
lemons	4	5	6	7	8
apple juice (unsweetened)	64 oz	80 oz	96 oz	112 oz	128 oz

A suggested division of responsibilities

Student A: steps 1, 6

Student B: steps 2, 7

Student C: steps 5, 8

Student D: steps 3, 4

Before class

1. Provide each group with 3 tea bags.

2. Provide each group with 6-8 mint stems, or enough to make $\frac{1}{2}$ cup leaves.

3. Provide each group with a lemon.

NOTE

1. Students can measure water and apple juice from the original containers.

Iced Apple-Mint Tea

Makes 4 Servings

Directions

Ingredients	

3 **orange-pekoe tea bags**

$\frac{1}{2}$ **cup fresh mint leaves**

1 lemon

2 cups boiling water

2 cups unsweetened apple juice

Utensils

pitcher

measuring cup

knife

cutting board

mixing spoon

strainer

Directions

_____ 1. Place **3 tea bags** in the pitcher.

_____ 2. Add $\frac{1}{2}$ **cup fresh mint leaves** to the pitcher.

_____ 3. Cut **lemon** in half. Add juice of half the lemon to the pitcher.

_____ 4. Slice the remaining half-lemon. Set slices aside to use when serving tea.

_____ 5. Measure **2 cups boiling water** into the pitcher. Let stand 5 minutes.

_____ 6. Measure **2 cups apple juice** into the pitcher. Stir.

_____ 7. Strain and serve over ice.

_____ 8. Garnish each glass with a lemon slice.

Light and Tasty Cooking Labs

Orange Nog

SHOPPING LIST

(4 students per group)	16 students	20 students	24 students	28 students	32 students
low-fat milk	2 qt	$2\frac{1}{2}$ qt	3 qt	$3\frac{1}{2}$ qt	4 qt
frozen orange-juice concentrate	16 oz	20 oz	24 oz	28 oz	32 oz
vanilla extract	8 tsp	10 tsp	3 tbsp	14 tsp	16 tsp
ice cubes	32	40	48	56	64

A suggested division of responsibilities

Student A: step 1

Student B: step 2

Student C: steps 3, 5

Student D: steps 4, 6

NOTES

1. Students can measure all ingredients from their original containers.

2. Students can get ice cubes from the freezer as needed. If cubes are too big for your blender, put them in a plastic bag and use a hammer to break cubes into smaller pieces.

Orange Nog

Makes 4 Servings

Directions

Ingredients

2 cups low-fat milk

$\frac{1}{2}$ **cup frozen orange-juice concentrate**

2 tsp vanilla extract

8 ice cubes

_____ 1. Measure **2 cups low-fat milk** into blender.

_____ 2. Measure $\frac{1}{2}$ **cup frozen orange-juice concentrate** into blender.

_____ 3. Measure **2 tsp vanilla extract** into blender.

_____ 4. Add **8 ice cubes** to blender.

_____ 5. Cover blender. Blend until smooth and foamy.

_____ 6. Serve immediately.

Utensils

blender
measuring cup
measuring spoon

Peach Smoothie

SHOPPING LIST

(4 students per group)	16 students	20 students	24 students	28 students	32 students
16-oz cans peaches (juice-packed)	4 cans	5 cans	6 cans	7 cans	8 cans
vanilla low-fat yogurt	48 oz	60 oz	72 oz	84 oz	96 oz
skim milk	24 oz	30 oz	36 oz	42 oz	48 oz
frozen apple-juice concentrate	4 oz	5 oz	6 oz	7 oz	8 oz
vanilla extract	2 tsp	$2\frac{1}{2}$ tsp	3 tsp	$3\frac{1}{2}$ tsp	4 tsp
ground nutmeg	16 shakes	20 shakes	24 shakes	28 shakes	32 shakes

A suggested division of responsibilities

Student A: steps 1, 5
Student B: steps 2, 6
Student C: steps 3, 7
Student D: steps 4, 8

Before class

1. Provide each group with a 16-oz can of peaches.

NOTE

1. Students can measure yogurt, milk, apple-juice concentrate, vanilla, and nutmeg from their original containers.

Peach Smoothie

Makes 4 Servings

Directions

<table>
<tr><td>

Ingredients

1 16-oz can peaches (packed in own juice)

$1\frac{1}{2}$ cups vanilla low-fat yogurt

$\frac{3}{4}$ cup skim milk

2 tbsp frozen apple-juice concentrate

$\frac{1}{2}$ tsp vanilla extract

ground nutmeg

</td></tr>
</table>

_____ 1. Drain **peaches**. Put peaches in blender.

_____ 2. Measure $1\frac{1}{2}$ **cups vanilla yogurt** into blender.

_____ 3. Measure $\frac{3}{4}$ **cup skim milk** into blender.

_____ 4. Measure **2 tbsp frozen apple-juice concentrate** into blender.

_____ 5. Measure $\frac{1}{2}$ **tsp vanilla extract** into blender.

_____ 6. Put cover on blender. Blend until smooth.

_____ 7. Pour into glasses.

_____ 8. Sprinkle each glass with **ground nutmeg**.

Utensils

can opener
blender
measuring cup
measuring spoons

             Light and Tasty Cooking Labs

Pink Drinks

SHOPPING LIST

(4 students per group)	16 students	20 students	24 students	28 students	32 students
low-calorie lemon-lime carbonated beverage	64 oz	80 oz	96 oz	112 oz	128 oz
10-oz packages frozen strawberries	4	5	6	7	8
pineapple juice (unsweetened)	16 oz	20 oz	24 oz	28 oz	32 oz

A suggested division of responsibilities

Student A: step 1
Student B: step 2
Student C: step 3
Student D: steps 4, 5

Before class

1. Provide each group with a 10-oz package of frozen strawberries.

NOTE

1. Students can measure lemon-lime beverage and pineapple juice from the original containers.

Pink Drinks

Makes 4 Servings

Directions

Ingredients

2 cups low-calorie lemon-lime carbonated beverage

1 10-oz package frozen strawberries

$\frac{1}{2}$ **cup unsweetened pine-apple juice**

_____ 1. Measure **2 cups low-calorie lemon-lime carbonated beverage** into the blender.

_____ 2. Add **frozen strawberries** to the blender.

_____ 3. Measure $\frac{1}{2}$ **cup pineapple juice** into the blender.

_____ 4. Cover blender and blend until smooth.

_____ 5. Serve immediately.

Utensils

blender

measuring cup

T. J. Pizzazz

SHOPPING LIST

(4 students per group)	16 students	20 students	24 students	28 students	32 students
tomato juice	64 oz	80 oz	96 oz	112 oz	128 oz
lemons	4	5	6	7	8
black pepper	1 tsp	$1\frac{1}{4}$ tsp	$1\frac{1}{2}$ tsp	$1\frac{3}{4}$ tsp	2 tsp
celery salt	1 tsp	$1\frac{1}{4}$ tsp	$1\frac{1}{2}$ tsp	$1\frac{3}{4}$ tsp	2 tsp
Worcestershire sauce	4 tsp	5 tsp	6 tsp	7 tsp	8 tsp
ice cubes	32-48	40-60	48-72	56-84	64-96
celery sticks	16	20	24	28	32

A suggested division of responsibilities

Student A: steps 1, 6, 11

Student B: steps 2, 3, 12

Student C: steps 4, 5, 13

Student D: steps 7, 8, 9, 10

Before class

1. Provide each group with a lemon.

2. Provide each group with 4 celery sticks.

NOTES

1. Students can measure tomato juice, black pepper, celery salt, and Worcestershire sauce from the original containers.

2. Students can get ice cubes from the freezer as needed.

T. J. Pizzazz

Makes 4 Servings

Directions

Ingredients
2 cups tomato juice
1 lemon
$\frac{1}{4}$ **tsp black pepper**
$\frac{1}{4}$ **tsp celery salt**
1 tsp Worcestershire sauce
8-12 ice cubes
4 celery sticks

_____ 1. Measure **2 cups tomato juice** into the jar.

_____ 2. Cut the **lemon** in half.

_____ 3. Squeeze the lemon juice into the jar.

_____ 4. Measure $\frac{1}{4}$ **tsp black pepper** into the jar.

_____ 5. Measure $\frac{1}{4}$ **tsp celery salt** into the jar.

_____ 6. Measure **1 tsp Worcestershire sauce** into the jar.

_____ 7. Put **8-12 ice cubes** in a plastic bag.

_____ 8. Wrap the bag of ice cubes in newspaper.

_____ 9. Pound the ice cubes with a hammer to make cracked ice.

_____ 10. Add the cracked ice to the jar.

_____ 11. Cover the jar and shake well.

_____ 12. Pour juice mixture into 4 glasses.

_____ 13. Garnish with a **celery stick** in each glass.

Utensils

1-qt jar with cover
measuring cup
paring knife
measuring spoons
plastic bag
newspaper
hammer

Desserts

Baked Apples

SHOPPING LIST

(4 students per group)	16 students	20 students	24 students	28 students	32 students
apples	16	20	24	28	32
light pancake syrup	4 oz	5 oz	6 oz	7 oz	8 oz
ground cinnamon	4 tsp	5 tsp	6 tsp	7 tsp	8 tsp
ground nutmeg	1 tsp	$1\frac{1}{4}$ tsp	$1\frac{1}{2}$ tsp	$1\frac{3}{4}$ tsp	2 tsp
granola cereal	1 cup	$1\frac{1}{4}$ cups	$1\frac{1}{2}$ cups	$1\frac{3}{4}$ cups	2 cups

A suggested division of responsibilities

Student A: steps 2, 3, 4 (with B & C), 8, 9
Student B: steps 2, 3, 4 (with A & C), 10
Student C: steps 2, 3, 4 (with A & B), 11
Student D: steps 1, 5, 6, 7

Before class

1. Provide each group with 4 apples.
2. Divide granola into $\frac{1}{4}$-cup packages and give each group a package.

NOTE

1. Students can measure pancake syrup, cinnamon, nutmeg, and water from the original containers.

Baked Apples

Makes 4 Servings

Directions

<table>
<tr><td>Ingredients</td></tr>
<tr><td>

4 baking apples

2 tbsp light pancake syrup

1 tsp cinnamon

$\frac{1}{4}$ **tsp nutmeg**

$\frac{1}{2}$ **cup water**

$\frac{1}{4}$ **cup granola cereal**

</td></tr>
</table>

_____ 1. Preheat oven to 350°.

_____ 2. Cut **4 apples** into quarters. Remove cores.

_____ 3. Slice apples into loaf pan.

_____ 4. Measure **2 tbsp light pancake syrup** into the bowl.

_____ 5. Measure **1 tsp cinnamon** into the bowl.

_____ 6. Measure $\frac{1}{4}$ **tsp nutmeg** into the bowl. Mix.

_____ 7. Measure $\frac{1}{2}$ **cup water** into the bowl. Mix well.

_____ 8. Pour the liquid over the apples.

_____ 9. Bake 20 minutes or until the apples are fork-tender.

_____ 10. Spoon baked apples into serving dishes.

_____ 11. Sprinkle **1 tbsp granola cereal** over each serving. Serve warm.

Utensils

loaf pan

cutting board

paring knife

small mixing bowl

measuring spoons

mixing spoon

Blueberry-Peach Cobbler à la Mode

SHOPPING LIST

(4 students per group)	16 students	20 students	24 students	28 students	32 students
apple juice	24 oz	30 oz	36 oz	42 oz	48 oz
cornstarch	$\frac{1}{4}$ cup	5 tbsp	6 tbsp	7 tbsp	$\frac{1}{2}$ cup
peaches	8	10	12	14	16
blueberries	4 cups	5 cups	6 cups	7 cups	8 cups
whole-wheat flour	2 cups	$2\frac{1}{2}$ cups	3 cups	$3\frac{1}{2}$ cups	4 cups
baking powder	1 tbsp	$3\frac{3}{4}$ tsp	$4\frac{1}{2}$ tsp	$5\frac{1}{4}$ tsp	2 tbsp
vanilla ice milk	2 pt	$2\frac{1}{2}$ pt	3 pt	$3\frac{1}{2}$ pt	4 pt

A suggested division of responsibilities

Student A: steps 1, 6, 15, 16

Student B: steps 2, 4, 5, 17, 18

Student C: steps 3, 7, 8, 9

Student D: steps 10, 11, 12, 13, 14

Before class

1. Provide each group with 2 peaches.

2. Divide blueberries into 1-cup packages and give a package to each group.

NOTES

1. Students can measure apple juice, cornstarch, flour, baking powder, and apple juice from the original containers.

2. Students can get ice milk from the freezer as needed.

Blueberry-Peach Cobbler à la Mode

Makes 4 Servings

Directions

Ingredients
$\frac{1}{2}$ cup apple juice
1 tbsp cornstarch
2 medium peaches
1 cup blueberries (fresh or frozen)
$\frac{1}{2}$ cup whole-wheat flour
$\frac{3}{4}$ tsp baking powder
$\frac{1}{4}$ cup apple juice
$\frac{1}{2}$ pt vanilla ice milk

Utensils

small saucepan
wooden spoon
measuring spoons
measuring cup
cutting board
paring knife
loaf pan
small bowl
mixing spoon

_____ 1. Preheat oven to 425°.

_____ 2. Measure $\frac{1}{2}$ **cup apple juice** into small saucepan.

_____ 3. Measure **1 tbsp cornstarch** into saucepan.

_____ 4. Cook over medium heat, stirring constantly.

_____ 5. Boil 1 minute and then remove from heat.

_____ 6. Cut **peaches** into quarters. Remove pits. Peel and chop peaches and add to saucepan.

_____ 7. Measure **1 cup blueberries** into saucepan.

_____ 8. Gently mix fruit.

_____ 9. Spoon fruit mixture into loaf pan.

_____ 10. Measure $\frac{1}{2}$ **cup whole-wheat flour** into small bowl.

_____ 11. Measure $\frac{3}{4}$ **tsp baking powder** into bowl.

_____ 12. Mix dry ingredients together.

_____ 13. Measure $\frac{1}{4}$ **cup apple juice** into bowl.

_____ 14. Mix just until dry ingredients are moistened.

_____ 15. Drop mixture by spoonfuls on friut.

_____ 16. Bake 20 minutes or until lightly browned.

_____ 17. Serve warm.

_____ 18. Spoon $\frac{1}{4}$ **cup ice milk** over each serving.

Chocolate Angel Food Cupcakes

SHOPPING LIST

(4 students per group)	16 students	20 students	24 students	28 students	32 students
cocoa	$\frac{3}{4}$ cup	15 tbsp	18 tbsp	21 tbsp	$1\frac{1}{2}$ cups
vanilla extract	1 tsp	$1\frac{1}{4}$ tsp	$1\frac{1}{2}$ tsp	$1\frac{3}{4}$ tsp	2 tsp
egg whites	8	10	12	14	16
sugar	$\frac{1}{2}$ cup	10 tbsp	$\frac{3}{4}$ cup	14 tbsp	1 cup
flour	$\frac{1}{2}$ cup	10 tbsp	$\frac{3}{4}$ cup	14 tbsp	1 cup
baking powder	4 tsp	5 tsp	6 tsp	7 tsp	8 tsp
confectioner's sugar	$\frac{1}{4}$ cup	5 tbsp	6 tbsp	7 tbsp	$\frac{1}{2}$ cup

A suggested division of responsibilities

Student A: steps 1, 3, 6, 15

Student B: steps 2, 4, 5, 14

Student C: steps 7, 9, 10, 16, 17

Student D: steps 8, 11, 12, 13, 18

Before class

1. Provide each group with 2 eggs.

NOTES

1. Students can measure cocoa, water, vanilla extract, sugar, flour, baking powder, and confectioner's sugar from the original containers.

2. Only the egg whites are used in this recipe.

Chocolate Angel Food Cupcakes

Makes 4 Cupcakes

Directions

Ingredients
3 tbsp cocoa
3 tbsp water
$\frac{1}{4}$ **tsp vanilla extract**
2 egg whites
2 tbsp sugar
2 tbsp flour
1 tsp baking powder
1 tbsp confectioner's sugar

Utensils

small saucepan
wooden spoon
measuring spoons
small bowl
mixer
rubber scraper
sifter
muffin tin
4 paper liners
strainer

_____ 1. Preheat oven to 350°.

_____ 2. Measure **3 tbsp cocoa** into saucepan.

_____ 3. Measure **3 tbsp water** into saucepan.

_____ 4. Heat cocoa and water over low heat for about 1 minute until mixture is smooth. Stir constantly.

_____ 5. Remove chocolate mixture from heat.

_____ 6. Measure $\frac{1}{4}$ **tsp vanilla extract** into chocolate mixture and stir.

_____ 7. Separate 2 eggs. Put **2 egg whites** in bowl.

_____ 8. Beat egg whites until soft peaks form.

_____ 9. Add **2 tbsp sugar** gradually, beating after each addition.

_____ 10. Add chocolate mixture to beaten egg whites. Beat just until blended.

_____ 11. Measure **2 tbsp flour** into sifter.

_____ 12. Measure **1 tsp baking powder** into sifter.

_____ 13. Sift dry ingredients into egg-white mixture.

_____ 14. Gently fold dry ingredients into egg-white-and-chocolate mixture.

_____ 15. Put paper liners into 4 muffin cups.

_____ 16. Divide batter into 4 muffin cups.

_____ 17. Bake 10 to 15 minutes, until paper liners pull away from sides of pan.

_____ 18. Put **1 tbsp confectioner's sugar** in the strainer and sprinkle over the cupcakes.

Citrus Cups

SHOPPING LIST

(4 students per group)	16 students	20 students	24 students	28 students	32 students
.3-oz pkg. sugar-free or regular gelatin (orange, lemon, or lime)	4	5	6	7	8
ice cubes	16-20	20-25	24-30	28-35	32-40
low-fat cottage cheese	2 cups	$2\frac{1}{2}$ cups	3 cups	$3\frac{1}{2}$ cups	4 cups
almond extract	2 tsp	$2\frac{1}{2}$ tsp	3 tsp	$3\frac{1}{2}$ tsp	4 tsp
oranges	4	5	6	7	8
slivered almonds	8 tbsp	10 tbsp	12 tbsp	14 tbsp	16 tbsp

A suggested division of responsibilities

> Student A: steps 1, 2, 7, 13
> Student B: steps 3, 4, 8, 9
> Student C: steps 5, 6, 11
> Student D: steps 10, 12, 14, 15

Before class

1. Provide each group with a package of gelatin.

2. Provide each group with an orange.

3. Divide almonds into packages of 2 tbsp each and give a packet to each group.

NOTE

1. Students can measure water, ice cubes, cottage cheese, and almond extract from the original containers.

Citrus Cups

Makes 4 Servings

Directions

Ingredients

$\frac{3}{4}$ cup boiling water

1 .3-oz pkg. sugar-free or regular gelatin (orange, lemon, or lime)

$\frac{1}{2}$ cup cold water

4-5 ice cubes

$\frac{1}{2}$ cup low-fat cottage cheese

$\frac{1}{2}$ tsp almond extract

1 large orange

2 tbsp slivered almonds

Utensils

saucepan

measuring cups

blender

measuring spoons

paring knife

4 dessert dishes

large spoon

_____ 1. Measure $\frac{3}{4}$ cup water into saucepan and bring to a boil.

_____ 2. Pour boiling water into blender.

_____ 3. Add **1 package sugar-free gelatin** to blender.

_____ 4. Cover blender and blend at low speed until gelatin is dissolved.

_____ 5. Combine **cold water** and **ice cubes** to make $1\frac{1}{4}$ cups and add to blender.

_____ 6. Cover blender and blend until cubes are partially melted.

_____ 7. Measure $\frac{1}{2}$ **cup low-fat cottage cheese** into blender.

_____ 8. Measure $\frac{1}{2}$ **tsp almond extract** into blender.

_____ 9. Cover blender and blend at high speed until smooth.

_____ 10. Peel **orange** and divide into sections. Cut each section into 3 or 4 pieces.

_____ 11. Half fill each dessert dish with gelatin mixture.

_____ 12. Add orange pieces to each dish.

_____ 13. Fill dishes with remaining gelatin.

_____ 14. Garnish desserts with slivered almonds.

_____ 15. Serve chilled.

Cream Puffs with Banana Filling

SHOPPING LIST

(4 students per group)	16 students	20 students	24 students	28 students	32 students
margarine	$\frac{1}{2}$ stick	5 tbsp	6 tbsp	7 tbsp	1 stick
flour	$1\frac{1}{3}$ cups	$1\frac{2}{3}$ cups	2 cups	$2\frac{1}{3}$ cups	$2\frac{2}{3}$ cups
eggs	8	10	12	14	16
ripe bananas	4	5	6	7	8
orange-juice concentrate	2 oz	$2\frac{1}{2}$ oz	3 oz	$3\frac{1}{2}$ oz	4 oz
low-calorie whipped topping	2 cups	$2\frac{1}{2}$ cups	3 cups	$3\frac{1}{2}$ cups	4 cups

2 **To use this recipe in a 2-day lab**
- On day 1, complete steps 1-13.
  Cool puffs and store in a covered container.
- On day 2, complete steps 14-20.

A suggested division of responsibilities

Student A: steps 1, 8, 9, 10

Student B: steps 2, 4, 11, 12, 13

Student C: steps 3, 5, 6, 7

Student D: steps 15, 16, 17, 18

All students take part in steps 14, 19, 20

Before class

1. Divide margarine into 1-tbsp chunks. Give a chunk to each group.

2. Provide each group with 2 eggs.

3. Provide each group with a banana.

NOTES

1. Students can measure water, flour, cream of tartar, and orange-juice concentrate from the original containers.

2. Students will have egg whites that will not be used in the recipe.

Cream Puffs with Banana Filling

Makes 4 Servings

Directions

Ingredients

1 tbsp margarine

$\frac{1}{3}$ **cup water**

$\frac{1}{3}$ **cup flour**

2 egg yolks

1 ripe banana

1 tbsp orange-juice concentrate

$\frac{1}{2}$ **cup low-calorie whipped topping**

Utensils

small saucepan

measuring cup

wooden spoon

fork

baking sheet

small bowl

measuring spoons

sharp knife

_____ 1. Preheat oven to 450°.

_____ 2. Measure **1 tbsp margarine** into saucepan.

_____ 3. Measure $\frac{1}{3}$ **cup water** into saucepan.

_____ 4. Heat water mixture to a boil.

_____ 5. Add $\frac{1}{3}$ **cup flour** to the water all at once, stirring vigorously.

_____ 6. Cook and stir until mixture forms a ball that stays together.

_____ 7. Remove from heat and let cool 2 to 3 minutes.

_____ 8. Separate the egg yolks from the egg whites. The egg whites will not be used in this recipe.

_____ 9. Add the **egg yolks** to the saucepan.

_____ 10. Beat until the dough is smooth and shiny. A fork may help in this process.

_____ 11. Drop dough on a baking sheet to form 4 puffs.

_____ 12. Bake for 15 minutes in a 450° oven.

_____ 13. Reduce heat to 325° and bake 10-12 minutes longer.

_____ 14. Cut off tops of cream puffs and remove soft centers.

_____ 15. Mash **banana** in small bowl.

_____ 16. Add **1 tbsp orange-juice concentrate** to banana.

_____ 17. Measure $\frac{1}{2}$ **cup whipped topping** into bowl.

_____ 18. Gently fold together banana mixture and whipped topping.

_____ 19. Spoon filling into cooled cream-puff bottoms.

_____ 20. Add tops and serve immediately.

Crunchy Fruit Parfait

SHOPPING LIST

(4 students per group)	16 students	20 students	24 students	28 students	32 students
oatmeal	$1\frac{1}{3}$ cups	$1\frac{2}{3}$ cups	2 cups	$2\frac{1}{3}$ cups	$2\frac{2}{3}$ cups
wheat germ	1 cup	$1\frac{1}{4}$ cups	$1\frac{1}{2}$ cups	$1\frac{3}{4}$ cups	2 cups
ground cinnamon	1 tsp	$1\frac{1}{4}$ tsp	$1\frac{1}{2}$ tsp	$1\frac{3}{4}$ tsp	2 tsp
pears	4	5	6	7	8
apples	4	5	6	7	8
bananas	4	5	6	7	8
oranges	4	5	6	7	8
kiwi fruit	8	10	12	14	16
lemon low-fat yogurt	32 oz	40 oz	48 oz	56 oz	64 oz
strawberries	16	20	24	28	32

A suggested division of responsibilities

Student A: steps 1, 2, 3, 4, 5, 6, 7, 18
Student B: steps 8, 13, 16, 17 (with C & D)
Student C: steps 9, 12, 15, 17 (with B & D)
Student D: steps 10, 11, 14, 17 (with B & C)

NOTES

1. Students can measure wheat germ, cinnamon, and yogurt from the original containers.

2. A variety of fruits can be used if some included in the recipe are not available.

Before class

1. Divide oatmeal into $\frac{1}{3}$-cup packages and give a package to each group.

2. Provide each group with a pear.

3. Provide each group with an apple.

4. Provide each group with a banana.

5. Provide each group with an orange.

6. Provide each group with 2 kiwi fruit.

7. Provide each group with 4 strawberries.

Crunchy Fruit Parfait

Makes 4 Servings

Directions

Ingredients

$\frac{1}{3}$ cup oatmeal

$\frac{1}{4}$ cup wheat germ

$\frac{1}{4}$ tsp cinnamon

1 pear

1 apple

1 banana

1 orange

2 kiwi fruit

1 cup lemon low-fat yogurt

4 strawberries

_____ 1. Preheat oven to 350°.

_____ 2. Measure $\frac{1}{3}$ **cup oatmeal** into small bowl.

_____ 3. Measure $\frac{1}{4}$ **cup wheat germ** into small bowl.

_____ 4. Stir oatmeal and wheat germ.

_____ 5. Spread mixture on a baking pan.

_____ 6. Bake 8-10 minutes, stirring occasionally, until mixture is lightly browned. Remove from oven.

_____ 7. Measure $\frac{1}{4}$ **tsp cinnamon** into oat mixture. Stir together.

_____ 8. Cut **pear** into quarters. Remove core. Chop pear and put in medium bowl.

_____ 9. Cut **apple**. Remove core. Chop apple and put in medium bowl.

_____ 10. Peel **banana**. Cut into thin slices and add to bowl.

_____ 11. Peel **orange**. Divide into sections. Cut each section in half. Add to bowl.

_____ 12. Peel **kiwi fruit**. Slice and add to bowl.

_____ 13. Mix the fruit gently.

_____ 14. Put a spoonful of fruit in the bottom of each parfait dish or glass.

_____ 15. Top fruit with a tbsp of **yogurt**.

_____ 16. Sprinkle with oat mixture.

_____ 17. Repeat layers 3 or 4 times, ending with oat mixture.

_____ 18. Top with a **strawberry**.

Utensils

small bowl

measuring cup

mixing spoon

baking pan

measuring spoons

medium bowl

cutting board

4 parfait dishes or wide-mouth glasses

paring knife

Fruit Tarts

SHOPPING LIST

(4 students per group)	16 students	20 students	24 students	28 students	32 students
pears or apples	4	5	6	7	8
brown sugar	$\frac{1}{4}$ cup	5 tbsp	6 tbsp	7 tbsp	$\frac{1}{2}$ cup
cinnamon	2 tsp	$2\frac{1}{2}$ tsp	3 tsp	$3\frac{1}{2}$ tsp	4 tsp
nutmeg	1 tsp	$1\frac{1}{4}$ tsp	$1\frac{1}{2}$ tsp	$1\frac{3}{4}$ tsp	2 tsp
lemon juice	2 tsp	$2\frac{1}{2}$ tsp	3 tsp	$3\frac{1}{2}$ tsp	4 tsp
eggs	4	5	6	7	8
puff pastry (frozen) 17-oz packages	2	$2\frac{1}{2}$	3	$3\frac{1}{2}$	4
flour	$\frac{1}{4}$ cup	5 tbsp	6 tbsp	7 tbsp	$\frac{1}{2}$ cup

A suggested division of responsibilities

Student A: steps 1, 8
Student B: steps 2, 7
Student C: steps 3, 4, 5, 6
Student D: steps 9, 10
All students take part in steps 11, 12, 13, 14, 15, 16, 17, 18, 19

Before class

1. Provide each group with 1 piece of fruit.
2. Provide each group with 1 egg.
3. Provide each group with one-half package of puff pastry.

NOTE

1. Students can measure brown sugar, cinnamon, nutmeg, lemon juice, and flour from their original containers.

Fruit Tarts

Makes 4 Servings

Ingredients

1 pear or apple

1 tbsp brown sugar

$\frac{1}{2}$ tsp cinnamon

$\frac{1}{4}$ tsp nutmeg

$\frac{1}{2}$ tsp lemon juice

$8\frac{1}{2}$-oz frozen puff pastry

1 tbsp flour

1 egg

Utensils

small bowl

paring knife

measuring spoons

mixing spoon

small dish

fork

pastry brush

baking sheet

Directions

_____ 1. Preheat oven to 375°.

_____ 2. Cut **fruit** into quarters. Remove core and chop fruit. Put chopped fruit in bowl.

_____ 3. Measure **1 tbsp brown sugar** into bowl.

_____ 4. Measure $\frac{1}{2}$ **tsp cinnamon** into bowl.

_____ 5. Measure $\frac{1}{4}$ **tsp nutmeg** into bowl.

_____ 6. Measure $\frac{1}{2}$ **tsp lemon juice** into bowl.

_____ 7. Mix ingredients in bowl.

_____ 8. Break **egg** into small dish. Beat with a fork.

_____ 9. Sprinkle **1 tbsp flour** on flat surface.

_____ 10. On floured surface, cut **pastry** into 8 squares.

_____ 11. Place spoonful of fruit mixture in center of four of the squares.

_____ 12. Brush edges of these four squares with beaten egg.

_____ 13. Top each pastry square with a second square.

_____ 14. Press edges with a fork to seal.

_____ 15. Use a sharp knife to make a small L-shaped cut in the center of each tart and fold back the flap so steam can escape.

_____ 16. Place tarts on the baking sheet.

_____ 17. Brush with beaten egg.

_____ 18. Bake 15-20 minutes until golden.

_____ 19. Serve warm or at room temperature.

Fruity Banana Split

SHOPPING LIST

(4 students per group)	16 students	20 students	24 students	28 students	32 students
bananas	8	10	12	14	16
ice milk	$\frac{1}{2}$ gal	5 pt	3 qt	7 pt	1 gal
strawberries	64	80	96	112	128
8-oz cans crushed pineapple (juice-packed)	4 cans	5 cans	6 cans	7 cans	8 cans

A suggested division of responsibilities

Student A: steps 1, 2

Student B: step 3

Student C: steps 4, 5

Student D: step 6

Before class

1. Provide each group with 2 bananas.

2. Provide each group with 16 strawberries.

3. Provide each group with an 8-oz can crushed pineapple.

NOTES

1. Students can get ice milk from the freezer as needed.

2. Have a variety of ice milk flavors so students can have a sample of several different flavors in their banana splits.

Fruity Banana Split

Makes 4 Servings

Directions

Ingredients		

2 bananas

1 pt ice milk

16 strawberries

1 8-oz can crushed pine-apple (packed in its own juice)

_____ 1. Peel **2 bananas** and cut in half.

_____ 2. Cut each half banana lengthwise to make 2 long pieces. Arrange 2 pieces of banana in each dish.

_____ 3. Measure $\frac{1}{2}$ **cup ice milk** into each dish.

_____ 4. Remove the hulls from **16 strawberries**.

_____ 5. Slice 4 strawberries over each dish of ice milk.

_____ 6. Spoon $\frac{1}{4}$ **cup crushed pineapple** and its juice over each banana split.

Utensils

knife

4 sauce dishes

spoon

can opener

Granola Cookies

SHOPPING LIST

(4 students per group)	16 students	20 students	24 students	28 students	32 students
margarine	2 sticks	$2\frac{1}{2}$ sticks	3 sticks	$3\frac{1}{2}$ sticks	4 sticks
brown sugar	1 cup	$1\frac{1}{4}$ cups	$1\frac{1}{2}$ cups	$1\frac{3}{4}$ cups	2 cups
small eggs	4	5	6	7	8
flour	1 cup	$1\frac{1}{4}$ cups	$1\frac{1}{2}$ cups	$1\frac{3}{4}$ cups	2 cups
baking soda	1 tsp	$1\frac{1}{4}$ tsp	$1\frac{1}{2}$ tsp	$1\frac{3}{4}$ tsp	2 tsp
granola	3 cups	$3\frac{3}{4}$ cups	$4\frac{1}{2}$ cups	$5\frac{1}{4}$ cups	6 cups

A suggested division of responsibilities

Student A: steps 1, 6, 7, 8

Student B: steps 2, 5

Student C: steps 3, 9

Student D: steps 4, 10

All students take part in steps 11, 12, 13

Before class

1. Provide each group with $\frac{1}{2}$ stick softened margarine.

2. Provide each group with an egg.

NOTES

1. Students can measure brown sugar, flour, baking soda, and granola from their original containers.

2. Depending on the ingredients in the granola used, you may also want to add: $\frac{1}{4}$ tsp cinnamon, $\frac{1}{8}$ tsp nutmeg, $\frac{1}{4}$ cup raisins, or $\frac{1}{4}$ cup chopped nuts.

Granola Cookies

Makes 1 Dozen Cookies

Directions

<table>
<tr><td></td></tr>
</table>

Ingredients
$\frac{1}{4}$ cup margarine, softened
$\frac{1}{4}$ cup brown sugar
1 small egg
$\frac{1}{4}$ cup flour
$\frac{1}{4}$ tsp baking soda
$\frac{3}{4}$ cup granola

Directions

_____ 1. Preheat oven to 350°.

_____ 2. Measure $\frac{1}{4}$ cup **margarine** into bowl.

_____ 3. Measure $\frac{1}{4}$ cup **brown sugar** into bowl.

_____ 4. Cream together until light and fluffy.

_____ 5. Add **egg** to bowl and mix well.

_____ 6. Measure $\frac{1}{4}$ cup **flour** into small bowl.

_____ 7. Measure $\frac{1}{4}$ tsp **baking soda** into small bowl.

_____ 8. Mix dry ingredients together.

_____ 9. Add dry ingredients to first bowl. Mix.

_____ 10. Measure $\frac{3}{4}$ cup **granola** and add to bowl. Mix thoroughly.

_____ 11. Drop cookies by the spoonful onto baking sheet.

_____ 12. Bake 10-12 minutes.

_____ 13. Cool on wire rack.

Utensils

medium bowl

measuring cups

mixing spoon

small bowl

measuring spoons

baking sheet

teaspoon

spatula

wire rack

Hot-Fudge Sundae

SHOPPING LIST

(4 students per group)	16 students	20 students	24 students	28 students	32 students
sugar	1 cup	$1\frac{1}{4}$ cups	$1\frac{1}{2}$ cups	$1\frac{3}{4}$ cups	2 cups
cocoa	1 cup	$1\frac{1}{4}$ cups	$1\frac{1}{2}$ cups	$1\frac{3}{4}$ cups	2 cups
low-fat milk	1 cup	$1\frac{1}{4}$ cups	$1\frac{1}{2}$ cups	$1\frac{3}{4}$ cups	2 cups
eggs	2	2	2	3	3
vanilla extract	1 tsp	$1\frac{1}{4}$ tsp	$1\frac{1}{2}$ tsp	$1\frac{3}{4}$ tsp	2 tsp
vanilla ice milk	4 pt	5 pt	6 pt	7 pt	8 pt
maraschino cherries	16	20	24	28	32

A suggested division of responsibilities

Student A: steps 1, 5, 10

Student B: steps 2, 6, 7

Student C: steps 3, 8, 11

Student D: steps 4, 9

Before class

1. Provide each group with 4 cherries.

NOTES

1. Break eggs into small dish and mix with a fork. Students can measure the required amount of egg from this dish.

2. Students can measure sugar, cocoa, milk, and vanilla extract from the original containers.

3. Students can get ice milk from the freezer as needed.

Hot-Fudge Sundae

Makes 4 Servings

Directions

Ingredients

$\frac{1}{4}$ **cup sugar**

$\frac{1}{4}$ **cup cocoa**

$\frac{1}{4}$ **cup low-fat milk**

1 tbsp egg

$\frac{1}{4}$ **tsp vanilla extract**

1 pt vanilla ice milk

4 maraschino cherries

_____ 1. Measure $\frac{1}{4}$ **cup sugar** into saucepan.

_____ 2. Measure $\frac{1}{4}$ **cup cocoa** into saucepan.

_____ 3. Measure $\frac{1}{4}$ **cup milk** into saucepan.

_____ 4. Measure **1 tbsp egg** into saucepan.

_____ 5. Mix all ingredients until smooth.

_____ 6. Place saucepan over very low heat. Bring to a near-boil, stirring constantly. Do not boil.

_____ 7. Remove from heat. Cool slightly.

_____ 8. Measure $\frac{1}{4}$ **tsp vanilla** into sauce. Mix well.

_____ 9. Spoon **ice milk** into 4 dessert dishes.

_____ 10. Pour sauce over ice milk.

_____ 11. Top each sundae with a **cherry**.

Utensils

small saucepan

measuring cups

measuring spoons

wooden spoon

4 dessert dishes

large spoon

Instant Strawberry Sherbet

SHOPPING LIST

(4 students per group)	16 students	20 students	24 students	28 students	32 students
vanilla-flavored instant-breakfast-drink powder	$\frac{1}{2}$ cup	10 tbsp	$\frac{3}{4}$ cup	14 tbsp	1 cup
20-oz packages frozen strawberries	4	5	6	7	8
vanilla extract	1 tsp	$1\frac{1}{4}$ tsp	$1\frac{1}{2}$ tsp	$1\frac{3}{4}$ tsp	2 tsp

A suggested division of responsibilities

Student A: steps 1, 5
Student B: steps 2, 6
Student C: step 3
Student D: step 4

Before class

1. Provide each group with a 20-oz package of frozen strawberries.

NOTES

1. Students can measure breakfast-drink powder and vanilla extract from the original containers.

2. A variety of other frozen fruits would work well in this recipe—try peaches or raspberries.

Instant Strawberry Sherbet

Makes 4 Servings

Directions

Ingredients

$\frac{1}{2}$ **cup water**

2 tbsp vanilla-flavored instant-breakfast-drink powder

1 20-oz package frozen strawberries

$\frac{1}{4}$ **tsp vanilla extract**

_____ 1. Measure $\frac{1}{2}$ **cup water** into blender.

_____ 2. Measure **2 tbsp vanilla-flavored instant-breakfast-drink powder** into blender.

_____ 3. Add **frozen strawberries** to blender.

_____ 4. Measure $\frac{1}{4}$ **tsp vanilla** into blender.

_____ 5. Cover blender and blend on high speed until smooth.

_____ 6. Spoon into dessert dishes and serve immediately.

Utensils

blender

measuring cup

measuring spoons

spoon

Light Chocolate Mousse

SHOPPING LIST

(4 students per group)	16 students	20 students	24 students	28 students	32 students
low-fat milk	$1\frac{1}{2}$ qt	1 qt, $3\frac{1}{2}$ cups	$2\frac{1}{4}$ qt	2 qt, $2\frac{1}{2}$ cups	3 qt
1.3-oz pkgs. chocolate sugar-free or regular instant pudding	4	5	6	7	8
low-calorie whipped topping	4 cups	5 cups	6 cups	7 cups	8 cups
strawberries	16	20	24	28	32

A suggested division of responsibilities

    Student A: steps 1, 5

    Student B: steps 2, 6

    Student C: steps 3, 7

    Student D: steps 4, 8

Before class

1. Provide each group with a package of pudding mix.

2. Provide each group with 4 strawberries.

NOTES

1. Students can measure milk and whipped topping from the original containers.

2. Be sure the whipped topping is thawed. Place it in the refrigerator the day before class.

Light Chocolate Mousse

Makes 4 Servings

Directions

Ingredients

$1\frac{1}{2}$ cups low-fat milk

1 1.3-oz pkg. chocolate sugar-free or regular instant pudding

1 cup low-calorie whipped topping (divided)

4 strawberries

Utensils

mixing bowl
measuring cups
wire whisk
4 dessert dishes
rubber scraper
large spoon

_____ 1. Measure $1\frac{1}{2}$ cups cold low-fat milk into a mixing bowl.

_____ 2. Sprinkle **1 pkg. chocolate pudding mix** over the milk.

_____ 3. Use wire whisk to combine the pudding mix and the milk.

_____ 4. Measure $\frac{3}{4}$ cup whipped topping into the bowl.

_____ 5. Using a rubber scraper, gently fold the whipped topping into the pudding.

_____ 6. Spoon mixture into 4 dessert dishes.

_____ 7. Spoon **1 tbsp whipped topping** on each serving.

_____ 8. Top each dessert with a strawberry.

Pear Crunch

SHOPPING LIST

(4 students per group)	16 students	20 students	24 students	28 students	32 students
pears	12	15	18	21	24
lemon juice	8 tsp	10 tsp	4 tbsp	14 tsp	16 tsp
almond extract	1 tsp	$1\frac{1}{4}$ tsp	$1\frac{1}{2}$ tsp	$1\frac{3}{4}$ tsp	2 tsp
flour	$\frac{1}{4}$ cup	5 tbsp	6 tbsp	7 tbsp	$\frac{1}{2}$ cup
dark brown sugar	$\frac{1}{4}$ cup	5 tbsp	6 tbsp	7 tbsp	$\frac{1}{2}$ cup
margarine	$\frac{1}{2}$ stick	5 tbsp	6 tbsp	7 tbsp	1 stick
oatmeal	$\frac{1}{2}$ cup	10 tbsp	$\frac{3}{4}$ cup	14 tbsp	1 cup

A suggested division of responsibilities

    Student A: steps 1, 8, 10, 12

    Student B: steps 7, 9, 11, 13

    Student C: steps 2 (with D), 3, 5

    Student D: steps 2 (with C), 4, 6

Before class

1. Provide each group with 3 pears.

2. Divide margarine into 1-tbsp chunks and give a piece to each group.

NOTE

    1. Students can measure lemon juice, almond extract, flour, brown sugar, and oatmeal from the original containers.

Pear Crunch

Makes 4 Servings

Directions

Ingredients
3 medium-size pears
2 tsp lemon juice
$\frac{1}{4}$ tsp almond extract
1 tbsp flour
1 tbsp dark brown sugar
1 tbsp margarine
2 tbsp oatmeal

_____ 1. Preheat oven to 375°.

_____ 2. Cut **pears** in quarters. Remove cores. Chop pears into small pieces. Put in medium bowl.

_____ 3. Measure **2 tsp lemon juice** into bowl.

_____ 4. Measure **$\frac{1}{4}$ tsp almond extract** into bowl.

_____ 5. Mix fruit with flavorings.

_____ 6. Divide fruit mixture among 4 custard cups.

_____ 7. Measure **1 tbsp flour** into small bowl.

_____ 8. Measure **1 tbsp dark brown sugar** into bowl.

_____ 9. Measure **1 tbsp margarine** into bowl.

_____ 10. Use your fingers to combine dry ingredients and margarine.

_____ 11. Measure **2 tbsp oatmeal** into crumb mixture and stir well.

_____ 12. Sprinkle crumb mixture over fruit.

_____ 13. Bake 15-20 minutes or until pears are tender.

Utensils

cutting board
knife
measuring spoons
medium bowl
4 custard cups
small bowl
mixing spoon

Light and Tasty Cooking Labs

Pineapple-Orange Pudding

SHOPPING LIST

(4 students per group)	16 students	20 students	24 students	28 students	32 students
16-oz cans crushed pineapple (juice-packed)	4 cans	5 cans	6 cans	7 cans	8 cans
plain low-fat yogurt	2 qt	$2\frac{1}{2}$ qt	3 qt	$3\frac{1}{2}$ qt	4 qt
orange-juice concentrate	8 oz	10 oz	12 oz	14 oz	16 oz
ice cubes	20	25	30	35	40
fresh mint leaves	16	20	24	28	32

A suggested division of responsibilities

Student A: steps 1, 6
Student B: steps 2, 7
Student C: step 3
Student D: step 4
All students take part in step 5

Before class

1. Provide each group with a 16-oz can of crushed pineapple.
2. Provide each group with 4 fresh mint leaves.

NOTES

1. Chill pineapple ahead of class time.
2. Students can measure yogurt and juice concentrate from the original containers.
3. Students can get ice cubes from the freezer as needed. If cubes are too big for your blender, put them in a plastic bag and use a hammer to break cubes into smaller pieces.

Pineapple-Orange Pudding

Makes 4 Servings

Directions

Ingredients
1 16-oz can crushed pineapple (packed in its own juice) **2 cups plain low-fat yogurt** $\frac{1}{4}$ **cup orange-juice concentrate** **5 ice cubes** **4 fresh mint leaves**

_____ 1. Pour **crushed pineapple** and its juice into blender.

_____ 2. Measure **2 cups yogurt** into blender.

_____ 3. Measure $\frac{1}{4}$ **cup orange-juice concentrate** into blender.

_____ 4. Cover and blend until smooth.

_____ 5. Add **ice cubes**, one at a time, blending after each addition, until chopped.

_____ 6. Pour into dessert dishes or glasses and garnish with **fresh mint**.

_____ 7. Serve chilled.

Utensils

blender
can opener
measuring cup
measuring spoons

Tropical Fruit Bowl

SHOPPING LIST

(4 students per group)	16 students	20 students	24 students	28 students	32 students
grapefruit	4	5	6	7	8
oranges	8	10	12	14	16
kiwi fruit	4	5	6	7	8
bananas	4	5	6	7	8
8-oz cans pineapple chunks (juice-packed)	4 cans	5 cans	6 cans	7 cans	8 cans
ground nutmeg	$\frac{1}{2}$ tsp	$\frac{5}{8}$ tsp	$\frac{3}{4}$ tsp	$\frac{7}{8}$ tsp	1 tsp
flaked coconut	$\frac{1}{2}$ cup	10 tbsp	$\frac{3}{4}$ cup	14 tbsp	1 cup

A suggested division of responsibilities

Student A: steps 1, 2, 9

Student B: steps 3, 4, 10

Student C: steps 5, 7, 11

Student D: steps 6, 8

Before class

1. Provide each group with a grapefruit.

2. Provide each group with 2 oranges.

3. Provide each group with a kiwi fruit.

4. Provide each group with an 8-oz can pineapple chunks.

5. Divide coconut into 2-tbsp packages and give a package to each group.

NOTES

1. Students can measure nutmeg from the original container.

2. Substitute or add other tropical fruits as they are available in your area.

Tropical Fruit Bowl

Makes 4 Servings

Directions

┌─────────────────────────────┐
│ *Ingredients* │
│ │
│ **1 grapefruit** │
│ │
│ **2 oranges** │
│ │
│ **1 kiwi fruit** │
│ │
│ **1 banana** │
│ │
│ **1 8-oz can pineapple chunks** │
│ **(packed in own juice)** │
│ │
│ $\frac{1}{8}$ **tsp nutmeg** │
│ │
│ **2 tbsp flaked coconut** │
└─────────────────────────────┘

Utensils

medium bowl

cutting board

knife

teaspoon

can opener

mixing spoon

measuring spoon

_____ 1. Cut **grapefruit** in half. Cut around fruit in each half.

_____ 2. Use a teaspoon to remove the grapefruit sections from the rind and place them in the bowl.

_____ 3. Peel the **orange**, removing the white pulp. Break the orange into sections.

_____ 4. Cut each orange section into 2 or 3 pieces. Remove all seeds. Add orange pieces to bowl.

_____ 5. Peel the **kiwi fruit**. Slice and add to bowl.

_____ 6. Peel the **banana**. Slice and add to bowl.

_____ 7. Add **8 oz pineapple** and the juice it is packed in.

_____ 8. Measure $\frac{1}{8}$ **tsp nutmeg**. Sprinkle it over the fruit.

_____ 9. Mix fruit gently.

_____ 10. Spoon into individual serving dishes.

_____ 11. Sprinkle with **flaked coconut**. Serve chilled.

What's Your Favorite Cooking Lab?

What do your students like to cook? What recipe works best with your foods classes?

Here's a chance to share your most successful lab with other foods teachers in the United States, Canada, and Australia. We're planning to publish a book of teachers' favorite cooking labs. If your recipe passes our taste and preparation tests, we'll include it as your favorite *and* send you a free copy of the book.

Send this completed form (or your own typewritten version) to:

Home Economics Editor
J. Weston Walch, Publisher
Box 658, 321 Valley Street
Portland, Maine 04104-0658

NAME OF RECIPE: _____ SERVINGS: _____

INGREDIENTS: _____ UTENSILS: _____

_____ _____

_____ _____

_____ _____

_____ _____

_____ _____

DIRECTIONS: _____

_____

_____

_____

_____

_____

Your name:

Your address:

Your school name:

Your school address:

Light and Tasty Cooking Labs